CALLING ALLAH
BY HIS MOST BEAUTIFUL NAMES

CALLING ALLAH
BY HIS MOST BEAUTIFUL NAMES

Shaykh Fadhlalla Haeri

Zahra Publications

Zahra Publications

First published in 2002 by
Zahra Publications

Distributed & Republished in 2018
Publisher: Zahra Publications
www.sfhfoundation.com
www.zahrapublications.com

© Shaykh Fadhlalla Haeri, 2018

All rights reserved. Except for brief quotations in critical articles or reviews, no part of this book may be reproduced in any manner without prior written permission from Zahra Publications.

Copying and redistribution of this Book is strictly prohibited.

Designed and typeset in South Africa by Quintessence Publishing
Cover Design by Quintessence Publishing

Set in 11 point on 15 point, Palatino Linotype
Printed and bound by Lightning Source

ISBN (Printed Version); Paperback: 978-1-928329-08-4

TABLE OF CONTENTS

Book Description	x
About the Author	xi
Editor's Note	xiii
Acknowledgment	xiv

PART I: FOUNDATIONS

Introduction	1
Unity (*Tawhid*)	6
References from the Qur'an	11
Prophetic Traditions	15
Etiquette of Du`ā	17
The Beautiful Names and Attributes	18
Best Times for Supplication	19
Special Places	20
When Supplication is Answered	21
Calling	23
Courtesies of Supplication	24
Supplication of Allah's Names and Attributes	26
The End – With Endless Beginnings	29
The Way Supplication Works	30

PART II: DIVINE PERFECTION

Introduction	33
The Eternal Quest	37

The Divine Names	40
Tradition and History of the Popular List of 99 Names	42
Exploring His Dominion	45
Allah's Beautiful Names and Attributes	46
1. ALLĀH	50
2. AL-RAHMĀN – The All-Merciful	51
3. AL-RAHĪM – The All-Compassionate	52
4. AL-MALIK – The King	53
5. AL-QUDDŪS – The Most Pure	54
6. AL-SALĀM – The Bestower of Peace	55
7. AL-MU'MIN – The Trustworthy	56
8. AL-MUHAYMIN – The Safeguarder	57
9. AL-`AZĪZ – The All-Mighty	58
10. AL-JABBĀR – The Compeller	59
11. AL-MUTAKABBIR – The Supremely Great	60
12. AL-KHĀLIQ – The Creator	61
13. AL-BĀRI' – The Maker	62
14. AL-MUSAWWIR – The Fashioner	63
15. AL-GHAFFĀR – The Coverer of all Faults	64
16. AL-QAHHĀR – The Subduer	65
17. AL-WAHHĀB – The Bestower	66
18. AL-RAZZĀQ – The Ever-Providing	67
19. AL-FATTĀH – The Opener	68
20. AL-`ALĪM – The All-Knowing	69
21. AL-QĀBID – The Restrictor	70
22. AL-BĀSIT – The Expander	71
23. AL-KHĀFID – The Debaser	72
24. AL-RĀFI` – The Exalter	73
25. AL-MU`IZZ – The Honorer	74
26. AL-MUDHILL – The Abaser	75

27.	AL-SAMĪ` – The All-Hearing	76
28.	AL-BASĪR – The All-Seeing	77
29.	AL-HAKAM – The Judge	78
30.	AL-`ADL – The All-Just	79
31.	AL-LATĪF – The Subtle	80
32.	AL-KHABĪR – The All-Cognizant	81
33.	AL-HALĪM – The Clement	82
34.	AL-`ADHĪM – The Magnificent	83
35.	AL-GHAFŪR – The All-Forgiving	84
36.	AL-SHAKŪR – The Grateful	85
37.	AL-`ALĪ – The Most High	86
38.	AL-KABĪR – The Incomprehensibly Great	87
39.	AL-HAFIDH – The Preserver	88
40.	AL-MUQĪT – The Sustainer	89
41.	AL-HASĪB – The Reckoner	90
42.	AL-JALĪL – The Majestic	91
43.	AL-KARĪM – The Most Generous	92
44.	AL-RAQĪB – The All-Vigilant	93
45.	AL-MUJĪB – The Responder	94
46.	AL-WĀSI` – The Vast	95
47.	AL-HAKĪM – The Most Wise	96
48.	AL-WADŪD – The All-Loving	97
49.	AL-MAJĪD – The Most Glorious	98
50.	AL-BĀ`ITH – The Resurrector	99
51.	AL-SHAHĪD – The All-Witnessing	100
52.	AL-HAQQ – The Absolute Truth	101
53.	AL-WAKĪL – The Guardian Trustee	102
54.	AL-QAWĪ – The Most Strong	103
55.	AL-MATĪN – The Firm	104
56.	AL-WALĪ – The Patron	105

57. AL-HAMĪD – The Praiseworthy	106
58. AL-MUHSI – The Appraiser	107
59. AL-MUBDĪ` – The Originator	108
60. AL-MU`ĪD – The Returner	109
61. AL-MUHYĪ – The Life-Giver	110
62. AL-MUMĪT – The Death-Giver	111
63. AL-HAYY – The Ever-Living	112
64. AL-QAYYŪM – The All-Sustaining	113
65. AL-WĀJID – The Manifestor	114
66. Al-Mājid – The Most Splendid	115
67. AL-WĀHID – The One	116
68. AL-AHAD – The Absolute One	117
69. AL-SAMAD – The Self-Sufficient	118
70. AL-QĀDIR – The Most Able	119
71. AL-MUQTADIR – The All-Powerful	120
72. AL-MUQADDIM – The Expediter	121
73. AL-MU'AKHKHIR – The Postponer	122
74. AL-AWWAL – The First	123
75. AL-ĀKHIR – The Last	124
76. AL-DHĀHIR – The Manifest	125
77. AL-BĀTIN – The Concealed	126
78. AL-WALĪ – The Governor	127
79. AL-MUTA`ĀLĪ – The Most Exalted	128
80. AL-BARR – The Benefactor	129
81. AL-TAWWAB – The Most Accepting of Repentance	130
82. AL-MUNTAQIM – He who brings about Trial and Affliction	131
83. AL-`AFŪW – The Pardoner	132
84. AL-RA'ŪF – The Most Affectionate	133

85. MĀLIK AL-MULK – The Master of The Kingdom   134
86. DHŪ AL-JALĀLI WA AL-IKRĀM – The Master of Majesty and Nobility   135
87. AL-MUQSIT – The All-Equitable   136
88. AL-JĀMI' – The Gatherer   137
89. AL-GHANI – The Rich Beyond Need   138
90. AL-MUGHNI – The Enricher   139
91. AL-MĀNI' – The Preventer   140
92. AL-DĀRR – The Bestower of Affliction   141
93. AL-NĀFI' – The Bestower of Benefit   142
94. AL-NŪR – The Light   143
95. AL-HĀDI – The Guide   144
96. AL-BADĪ' – The Innovator   145
97. AL-BĀQI – The Everlasting   146
98. AL-WĀRITH – The Inheritor   147
99. AL-RASHĪD – The Most Discerning   148
100.   AL-SABŪR – The Patient   149
101.   AL-RABB – The Lord   150

Divine Names Not Used in Tirmidhi's/Al-Ghazali's Lists   151
Compound Names   154

PART III: ADDITIONS

Introduction   157
Relevant Āyāt from the Qur'an   159
Relevant Prophetic Teachings   163
Few Special *Du'ā*   168
Selected Part of the Haydari Wird (Litany)   171
Glossary of Terms   175

BOOK DESCRIPTION

The primal design of human beings is based on an intrinsic knowledge of perfection and its yearning and journeying towards it. Life's experience is based on polarities and opposites, all of which is founded on a zone of constancy that does not change. All needs and desires are drives toward the perfection of the highest. The intelligent human being has no choice other than calling on Allah, whose Most Beautiful Names and Attributes are perfect at all times. It is by that calling and worship that we achieve the fruits of existence.

"In this book, we have presented a brief discourse on the doors of entry into the vast, boundless divine light created through supplication and calling upon Allah. Our hope is to facilitate its use, benefit and transformation for the traveler along the path. Thus, the repeated reading and use of this book by the seeker is recommended to open up the numerous horizons and subtleties of Allah's ways of grace."

– from the Introduction by Shaykh Fadhlalla Haeri

ABOUT THE AUTHOR

Shaykh Fadhlalla Haeri is a spiritual philosopher and writer whose role as a teacher grew naturally out of his own quest for self-fulfillment. Since childhood he has been attracted to scientific investigation and intellectual pursuit. He was born in Karbala, Iraq, and is a descendant of several generations of well-known and revered spiritual leaders.

After a stint in industry and consulting, he embarked on teaching, writing and meditating.

His awareness of global realpolitik compelled him to seek a truth that would reconcile the past with the present, the East and West. His discovery affirms that One Cosmic Reality is the source behind all known and unknown states.

Shaykh Haeri's unifying perspective emphasizes practical, actionable knowledge of self-transformation. It provides a natural bridge between different approaches to spirituality, offering common ground of higher knowledge for various religions, sects and secular outlooks.

His main work has been to make traditional Islamic teachings more comprehensible and widely available to the modern seeker through courses and publications. Shaykh Fadhlalla Haeri is currently engaged in lecturing and writing books and commentaries on the Holy Qur'an and related subjects, with particular emphasis on ethics, self-development and gnosis (*'irfan*).

With a lifetime's experience of contemplation, research,

and insights, he shares what it means to live in the light of the Absolute in a relative world and maintains that spiritual awakening is potentially available to all.

EDITOR'S NOTE

A standard form of transliteration has been used throughout the book, with only one exception: the letter ظ has been rendered as *dh* (Al-Adhīm, Al Hafidh, Al-Dhāhir), for though it may be mistaken for ذ, it was felt that the standard *z* might be more misleading, especially as no diacritic dots have been included to distinguish it.

ACKNOWLEDGMENT

The first printing of this book was produced with the help of so many people over the course of several years. The following friends and family deserve a special mention: Zainab Hussein Haeri; Muna Bilgrami; Abdul Hadi Bengt Stendlert; Aliya B. Haeri; Yahya, Ali and Ahmed Haeri, Azra Bilgrami Liden and Yunus Ismail.

Special thanks are due to Sayyed Jafar Kashfi, master calligrapher, who produced the beautiful calligraphy exclusively for this book. The printing of this edition of the book was produced with the help of Ebrahim Variawa, Safiyyah Surtee and Leyya Kalla.

PART I
FOUNDATIONS

INTRODUCTION

Allah created in order to be worshipped, praised, glorified and thus known. He is the source and the destination, He is the ever-present. Knowledge of Allah's ways, laws of creation and decrees are therefore essential for a harmonious journey towards an enlightened destiny.

> In a divinely revealed tradition (*hadīth qudsi*),
> Allah said:
> *I was a hidden treasure and I loved to be known,
> so I created.*

Thus the ultimate station of life's journey is to discover the ever-present treasure through love and submission.

True understanding of Allah's ways and His will can be achieved through submission (*islām*) and faith (*īmān*), and by prayers, calling unto Him and supplication (*du`ā*). Allah in His perfect design and mercy created needs, shortages and desires. He did this so that people would be reminded of dependency and submission to their Creator and Sustainer, Who alone can alleviate shortcomings, ward off evils and afflictions and bring in desirable success. Returning to Him through submission, fearful awareness (*taqwā*), and illumined faith, we experience His great compassion and perfect decrees. With restrictions and afflictions, one is humbled and brought to experience the gift of patience and trust in Him. In this way harmony is established in life.

The realization of total dependence on Allah is the starting point in awareness of His unique and eternal supremacy and might, as well as His compassion and perfect design for humankind's sustainable happiness through worship (`ibādah`). The path will lead to the realization of the true nature of the human being: an eternal spirit (*rūh*) activating a soul or self (*nafs*) in need of grooming and sublimation.

Prayers, supplication (*du`ā*) and calling upon Allah are the foundation upon which we develop our faith (*īmān*) and excellence (*ihsān*), leading to Heightened knowledge of Allah and transformative worship (`ibādah`). Through this joyful action, new horizons of understanding and the unveiling of truths and knowledges will take place. Thus transformation will lead to the discovery of our divine origin within, the spirit (*rūh*).

Allah reveals in the Qur'an and the way (*sunnah*) of His prophets and messengers that the path to happiness begins with fearful awareness, repentance and the return to Him. The human spirit in us has descended to the world of physical and existential realms to illuminate the self (*nafs*) and, through it; the body, mind and all the senses. Only then can the Adamic self ascend again to the abode of the Garden, both here and in the Hereafter. Transformation of the self occurs when it is restricted, purified, cleansed and emptied of its wayward, lower tendencies and then tethered to the tight rope of ascension, whose fabric is adoration, remembrance of God (*dhikr*), prayer, supplication, and sincere reliance and unconditional trust in Allah. This is called the religion (*Dīn*) of Allah: the natural way to be and interact.

Since the dawn of Islam, many Muslim scholars and

shuyookh have written about supplication and have used the Divine Names and Attributes as invocations. The Qur'an reveals that all power belongs to Allah, and the qualities of majesty, glory and praiseworthiness are His. The truth of unity is that Allah is the source behind every manifestation and meaning of events. Appropriate and transformative worship will lead us to the supreme one source behind all creation, which appears in pairs, opposites and infinite diversities. The garden is one. The same water, the same sun and the same air produce infinite varieties of flowers and shrubs.

Allah's great Names and Attributes are clearly signposted doors to His effulgence, mercy and generosity. When one is suffering from physical illness, for example, it is quite natural to seek healing, thus calling upon the Healer, Al-Shāfī (Qur'an 26:80). When one is confused by different choices and possible conflicting action, one calls upon Al-Hādi, the Guide. Then the door of Al-Fattāh, the Opener, is knocked upon when one is confined by and restricted in life's possibilities. The courtyard of Al-Rahmān, the All-Merciful, is the widest and most open to all creation, at all times.

Over the past centuries several lists of Divine Names and Attributes have been popularized and circulated among Muslims. Most of these lists have their origin in a Prophetic tradition, which relates that to Allah belong 99 Names, and whoever counts them will enter the Garden.

There are, however, a few variations in the lists of the 99 Divine Names attributed to the Prophet, peace and blessings be upon Him.[1] Enlightened scholars and commentators emphasize, therefore, the importance

---

1   It is customary, whenever the Prophet's name is mentioned, to invoke the traditional supplication of, "peace and blessings be upon him." In the remainder of the text, the invocation will appear in its abbreviated form, as (*pbuh*).

of understanding the Name or the Attribute, and the appropriate supplication by it, rather than the list itself.

As supplication is a foundation of the religion of Islam, it is no wonder that many books and discourses on it have accumulated throughout the Muslim world. Supplications, prayers and remembrance of Allah and His Attributes have indeed become an integral part of everyday Muslim life. In this book we have presented a brief discourse on the doors of entry into the vast, boundless divine light created through supplication and calling upon Allah. Our hope is to facilitate its use, benefit and transformation for the traveler along the path. The chapters are brief, yet contain broad and profound dimensions. Thus the repeated reading and use of this book by the seeker is recommended to open up the numerous horizons and subtleties of Allah's ways of grace.

Although this is a new and original book written in the English language and for the modern reader, its contents are rooted in Islam original: the true universal Prophetic path. The map of our path of Islam is based on the Qur'an, the Prophetic way, and the teachings from reliable and readily available source books, the Prophetic household and the great scholars and famous shuyookh of the path of sobriety. Ultimately the perfect model and universal being worthy of being followed is Muhammad (*pbuh*). References from the Qur'an and the Prophetic teachings are collected and listed in Part III of the book, rather than in the text of Parts I and Parts II, to ease the flow of reading for the general reader.

Allah is the true guide and we submit to Him with joy and contentment. He is the originator and the destiny. By Him the wayfarer starts and to Him is the return. No strength and no power, except by Allah. There is no God, but Allah, and Muhammad is His Prophet. (*Lā hawlah wa lā quwwata illā billāh. La ilāha illā Allah Muhammadun Rasūl Allah*).

UNITY (TAWHID)

In truth there is none except the One – Allah. All other short-lived realities exist by the grace of the unique One. All creation is originated from Him, sustained by Him and to Him is their return, the supreme Light of lights.

Allah describes Himself in the Qur'an as:

The Light of the heavens and the earth Allah! There is no God but Him, the Ever-Living, the Self-Subsisting.
Neither slumber nor sleep overtakes Him. To Him belongs whatever is in the heavens and in the earth.
Who can intercede with Him except by His permission. He knows what is before them and what is behind them, while they cannot contain anything of His Knowledge except what He wills.
His Footstool encompasses the heavens and the earth, and He is never weary of preserving them. He is the Most High, the Magnificent.
(2:255)

Allah is the unique name of God. A name is the means by which you point out an entity either because of an attribute specific to it or because it is singularly unique.

Allah is the absolute necessary being and the only constant truth behind all changing realities. All manifestations, experiences and existences are subject to change and uncertainty. By reference to the One, a better understanding of duality and multiplicity can be achieved. An easier journey and safer arrival will be experienced.

The significance and uniqueness of the Divine Name, Allah, is that it is the supreme essence described by the attribute of Divinity (*Ulūhiyyah*), and known by the quality of Lordship (*Rubūbiyyah*), characterized by the attribute of His oneness (*Ahadiyyah*) and singular unique unity, qualified by everlasting eternity, transcending all manner of description and comparison. He is sanctified beyond any point at which human intelligence can comprehend.

All of Allah's Names indicate His pure essence or an essence with an attribute in it, such as Al-Rahmān, the All-Merciful, indicating the root of mercy (*rahmah*), as well as the quality of mercy. The Names are either a pure Name or a derived Name. However, all the beautiful Names or Attributes relate and emanate from His essence (*dhāt*).

Allah says in the Qur'an:

The seven heavens and the earth and everyone in them glorify Him. There is nothing which does not glorify Him with His praise, but you do not understand their glorification.
He is All-Forbearing, Ever-Forgiving.
(17:44)
Everything in the heavens and everything in the earth glorifies Allah.
He is the Almighty, the All-Wise.
(59:1)

Thus every creation known and unknown is responding to its Originator's purpose for its existence and, by His plan and design, sings His glory.

In the case of human beings there are numerous ways and doors that open up for worship and glorification, and the seeker needs to knock at the most appropriate door, as the occasion arises. What matters most is sincerity, purity and presence of heart. For the contented and sensitive believer (*mu'min*), whatever manifests from the Beloved is a gift of love and mercy even though it may appear in the form of constriction or affliction. Every experience contains within it a reminder to remember Him.

The three main realms of unity relate to the zones of action, attribute and essence. Action and manifestation are based on causality, reasoning and intellect. The reflective believer will soon discover that all experiences are balanced by their opposites. There is no pleasure without displeasure, no Health without illness, and the root of these realities lies in their opposite. Higher attributes reflect the divine qualities and are most desirable for us as they are doors to inner happiness. Essence is the indiscernible and hidden root – the Light of lights. When one is illumined, the state of excellence (*ihsān*) is experienced and tasted. Then the All-Merciful appears and you will see His light in every situation.

The highest and subtlest realm of creation is called the *Jabarūt*, and it is the realm of essence, of pure light, primal energy and power. The *Malakūt* is the realm of attributes, of the angels, devils (*shaytans*) and other invisible entities. The realm of the *Mulk* is the phenomenal world of action and manifestation – our discernible universe.

As life in our discernible world is based on action, it means we live with constant change; hence we are always seeking a reliable zone of reference so that we can understand change and deal with it with a sense of priority. We may desire a beautiful object, for example, but it can deteriorate and become ugly in time or under certain circumstances. Thus, what we really desire is the attribute of beauty, and not the object itself.

The realm of attributes is subtler than that of the realm of action and manifestation. Even subtler is the essence of Allah which is hidden in His attributes, which themselves are behind the actions and manifestations of physical existence. Therefore, witnessing and understanding the unity of action and manifestation comes before realizing the unity of attributes, all of which meet in the one essence.

The Prophet (*pbuh*) said:

> I take refuge in Your forgiveness from Your punishment [unity of actions] and take refuge in Your mercy from Your anger [unity of attributes] and I take refuge in You from You. [unity of essence] Oh Lord, do not let me rely upon myself, not even for a blink of an eye.

Its meaning is that there is only 'You' behind all that appears, and within all that there is. 'You' are the outer and the inner.

Everything in existence has its potential capability and uniqueness which distinguishes it from every other creation. It is towards this potential that all creation is driven by the two forces of attraction (of desirables) and repulsion (of detestables). Everything in existence strives to reach its perfection through the realization of self-contentment and happiness by following its purpose and reaching its goal. In the case of human beings, it is the divine spirit within that is beckoning us to rise out of dense matter back to the subtle and heavenly origin from where we descended – the abode of the lights and spirits. The Adamic descent, an apparent separation from the divine essence, is the driving force behind awakening and the inner realization through illumined ascent, by the grace of Him Who was never separate and in Whose power lie the highest abodes as well as the lowest domains.

By Allah we have come into this existence and by Allah we travel unto Him. There is none other than Him and the multitudes of creation testify to His Supreme Oneness. Apparent multiplicity only proves His Unicity. The supplication of the believer is like the song of the reed, calling for and yearning for its original home, the reed bed. Human beings recall the original Adamic garden where the One Light shone and no shadows existed – the true eternal Garden.

All real spiritual endeavors and struggles relate to the secrets and metaphysical challenge of unity and oneness within infinite varieties of manifestation. The ocean is one, while the fish living in it are of infinite color and variety. There is no God but Allah, and Muhammad is His Prophet. *Lā ilāha illā Allah Muhammadun Rasūl Allah.*

REFERENCES FROM THE QUR'AN

The Qur'an is the revealed code, message and way of Allah regarding His Creation, it is His intention, will, commands, prohibitions, and patterns governing the cosmos. It is the 'gathered' depository of all knowledge, wisdom, remedies, tonics and secrets of lights and spiritual agencies. It is the divine treasury and the ultimate reference point in the journey to truth.

The Qur'an declares that Adam is Allah's deputy on earth and as such is responsible for his actions and will be rewarded accordingly. Thus we have a choice of godliness (*taqwā*) or depravity (*fujūr*), and as such prepare the way for the Garden or for Hell. Both of these states are also Here on earth as a prelude and paradigm for the Hereafter.

To prepare ourselves for transformation and for the realization of the purpose of our creation we need to recognize the lower human tendencies and deal with these by grooming and controlling the self. Consistent disciplined actions according to the code of conduct (*sharī`ah*) are needed. Accountability to enlightened teachers and true followers of the Prophetic path will bring about reflectiveness and heightened awareness, both for individuals as well as society. The Qur'anic lights and wisdom; and the Prophetic path prescribe Allah and the Prophetic practice (*sunnah*). These are the natural and primal latent patterns, the original, divine blueprint (*fitrah*), within the human soul.

Allah reveals in the Qur'an that the purpose of the Adamic creation, which is awakening to real life, will only be realized by humility, submission to the truth, and illumined faith, through acts of worship, such as prayer, fasting and supplication.

The Qur'an mentions the word supplication (*du`ā*) and its derivatives in numerous verses. The meaning of supplication relates to: calling, addressing, invoking and imploring. The relevant references to calling and supplication are listed in Part III of the book. The Qur'an contains numerous verses regarding different approaches and guidelines, as well as texts for supplication. A few of these are selected and included in Part III.

Allah enjoins His creation to call on Him and remember Him at all times. He commands to be called with humility and innermost sincerity and yearning. He also promises that if you call truly, He will answer.

Allah reminds the weak Adamic tribe on earth that they call on Him when desperate and desist when content. His mercy is such that He signals to His creation the need to submit and remember by bringing about scarcity, difficulties and tribulations. Otherwise creation will not heed and accept His will. Thus He created the needs for supplication and the appropriate preparedness for it, such as cautious awareness, reliance on and trust in His perfect nurturing and gentleness.

He also reminds us that rewards and openings are according to effort in the way of truth and that the purpose of this life is to strive towards knowledge of Him and towards the realization of His eternal presence. In this way supplication brings about heightened remembrance of Him.

As for calling upon His Glorious Names and Attributes, He commands us to call upon the gate of mercy. His mercy encompasses all manifestations, existences and experiences. Human affliction and trouble are marks of transgression, distraction and errors to be avoided. Thus repentance is the key to future ease and contented harmony with His decrees. His mercy covers adversity as well as good fortune. His mercy includes our realization of wrongdoing and repentance, and the ability to perform worship and supplication.

The Qur'an mentions numerous Names and Attributes of Allah. There is no fundamental difference between a name and an attribute, except that a name indicates an essence, such as Al-Hayy, The Ever-Living, and Al-`Alim, The All-Knowing, while an attribute implies action with essence in it, such as Al-Razzāq, The Ever-Providing, and Al-Hādi, The Guide. There is no doubt that the Divine Names and Attributes vary to the extent of the domain they cover and their specificity or generality. For example, Al-Rahmān, The All-Merciful, is the most comprehensive attribute, whereas Al-Nāsir, The Giver of Victory, is a very specific attribute both in terms of time and activity.

The Qur'an declares that all great, glorious and beautiful attributes belong to Allah, and that as part of human need and worship these qualities are to be called on as signposts towards human fulfillment through protection and forgiveness (*ghufrān*). For example, when we call upon the All-Generous, or Al-Karīm, His Light will cover our meanness. His Attribute of patience, *Al-Sabur*, when called upon, can envelop all of our impatience.

Allah warns against extreme deviation and associating anything with Allah, and His injunction is to acknowledge shortcomings, needs and dependence upon the Creator, whose primary purpose of creation is knowledge and worship, based on unity.

Creation is at all times under the control of Allah, the All-Mighty, the Merciful and the Ever-Present. Allah draws us close to Him through our needs and inadequacies so that we may come to realize His perfection and absoluteness. The seeker's appropriate response is to call upon the desirable Name, Attribute or any appropriate supplication, that will take him or her close to the divine precinct from which all mercy emanates and engulfs creation.

Allah's purpose in creating is for Him to be worshipped, prayed to and known. We can progress on this path through a deeper knowledge of His ways and attributes through the doors that lead to Him. The Beautiful Names are the doors which will unlock with the keys of submission, genuine need, reliance and trust in His generous answer.

The Qur'an is the source book of unity and when we follow its light, and listen to it and yield to it truly, we begin to realize the depth and transformative light of "There is no God, but Allah and Muhammad is His Prophet" *Lā ilāha illā Allah Muhammadun Rasūl Allah*.

PROPHETIC TRADITIONS

In Arabic the word *nabī*, prophet, is from the root word which means news, view or insight. The word *rasūl* is from the root word meaning message, letter, instruction or commands. Our Prophet Muhammad (*pbuh*) was both a prophet and a messenger. His message was based on unity and his news was based on the truth which leads to self-realization, to lasting inner contentment based on faith, fearful awareness, and the knowledge of Allah's perfect ways and designs. Muhammad's (*pbuh*) life, conduct and most perfect and natural ways were described as the 'Living Qur'an'.

The Prophetic teachings and practices are very rich regarding the importance of supplication and prayers to Allah and calling upon His Attributes and Beautiful Names. The Prophet (*pbuh*) recommended prayers and supplications for specific times and certain circumstances, which are described later in this chapter.

The Prophet (*pbuh*) has taught that:
- Supplication is itself worship.
- Supplication is the core of worship.
- Nothing will change one's destiny except supplication and prayers.
- Supplication from the slave to his Lord is one of his key duties and one of his greatest

obligations.
- Supplication is the weapon of the believer; the foundation of religion and the light of the heavens and earth.

Supplication does not contradict the caller's state of contentment and inner ease. The blessed Prophet (*pbuh*) himself constantly called upon Allah, and encouraged repeating the supplication and persisting in prayer. He confirmed that Allah will deposit His gifts into the outstretched arms in prayer. He also discouraged people from asking of other human beings by saying that:

You repel people by asking them, whilst you draw closer to Allah by asking Him. (2:216)

This does not imply that one is not grateful for human kindness and consideration. The believer regards all creation as means and instruments of the Creator, under His control. To realize this truth, first accept it on trust and then you will witness its truth and be transformed through surrender (*islām*), faith (*īmān*) and excellence (*ihsān*). We need the Prophetic example and perfection as a model to live by. Without loving the Prophet (*pbuh*) and believing in his just vicegerency (*Khilafah* of Allah) our progress will be faulty.

A useful paradigm is the hologram. If we groom the *nafs* on the model of the Prophetic conduct and *Dīn*, the hologram "I" is most prepared to be transformed by the truth, to be enlightened and witness the Light of The Supreme One – a small mirror reflecting the original Light of the Creator.

Etiquette of Du`ā

Regarding the etiquette (*adab*) of *du`ā* and calling Allah, the Prophet (*pbuh*) advised:
- Do not be hesitant or uncertain in your *du`ā*.
- Do not be disappointed if your call is not answered by the time you expect it; it may be saved for you. 'Delay is not denial.'
- Repeat and persist in your calls, for he who knows Allah the most will ask Him for the most, and most frequently.
- Do not belittle the calls of others to Allah. He may answer the call of those you do not consider worthy of being answered.

As for unanswered calls we are told that the reason can include:
- The caller had not despaired from other people's help and was not truly in need or desperate, and thus not single-minded or focused in his calling upon Allah. Lack of sincerity and dependence on Allah is a big barrier.
- A call is not answered because the caller is not in *tawḥīd* and is not able to address or reach whom he is calling. This lack of deep courtesy will affect the appropriate transmission of the *du`ā*.
- The caller has a very short-term need or desire and does not know what is really best for him in the longer term. Allah declares in the Qur'an:
  And it may be a good thing for you, but you detest it, and it may be wrong for you, and you desire it.

- The caller has not persisted enough in his calling, is impatient, or lacks certainty of the answer. He may also not be sure of, or clear in, what is needed.

The Beautiful Names and Attributes

Allah's most Beautiful Names have been endorsed in numerous books and compilations on the Prophetic tradition. One famous and popularly quoted Prophetic tradition of the Divine Names and Attributes is that: *'Allah has 99 Names and whoever counts them will enter the Garden.'* This tradition has often been quoted with slight variation by respected scholars, but essentially with the same meaning. These 99 Names are detailed in books by Tirmidhi, Ibn Majah, Hakim and others, and mostly originate from a tradition by Abu Hurairah, as well as others.

The Prophetic tradition does not restrict Allah's Names and Attributes to 99, but its emphasis is on counting, reciting, understanding, and recalling these Names. The Arabic word in this tradition is translated as 'counting' which also means to learn, memorize, reflect upon and gather (the meaning and connotation of these Names). Some commentators even highlight the need to apply the Name or Attribute to oneself, live by it, and visualize it so as to get closer to its deep meaning and implication for conduct.

The Prophet (*pbuh*) has said:

No one will ever be grieved if he asks Allah by every Name that belongs to Him, that He has called Himself by, or has brought down in His book, or has taught to any of His creation.

This means that Allah's Names and Attributes are far greater in power than we know or can relate to.

Best Times for Supplication

Every aspect in life undergoes dual cycles which connect, such as ebbing and flowing, expansion and contraction, rising and falling, living and dying. The season to plant is spring, when growth and expansion are most conducive naturally. In winter most plants contract and stop growing. As every action has a favorable time; so too does supplication, the timing of which relates to the state of the caller as well as the circumstances. Also there are naturally occurring periods during the year when planetary positions, electromagnetic fields, and other conditions, are most favorable.

The following is a brief list of favorable 'calendar' times for supplication:

- The Night of Power or Determination (*Laylat al-Qadr*), during the Fasting month of Ramadan
- The Day of `*Arafāt* of the Hajj (Pilgrimage)
- The Month of Ramadan
- Any Thursday Night
- Any Friday, during the day
- The middle of the night
- Before dawn (*fajr*)
- The last third of the night
- When the prayer (*salāt*) is called – the short interval between the call to prayer (*adhān*) and beginning the prayer
- Immediately after the prayer (*salāt*)
- During prostration (*sajdah*)

- During a gathering for the remembrance of God (*dhikr*)
- During a rainstorm and other unusual earthly events such as earthquakes or tornadoes
- At the time of death of a believer (*mu'min*)
- At the time of birth
- And other occasions of special or personal significance

The Prophet (*pbuh*) has said that:

Three supplications will be clearly answered: At the time when a person is breaking his fast, when a pious and just spiritual leader (*imam*) makes supplication, and when an unjustly treated person calls out to Allah for help.

Ultimately the condition and state of the caller dictates the appropriate time to call. A pure heart, a clear and dedicated disposition, a sincere and desperate need, and high expectation of Allah, fear of Him and unconditional love and trust in Him all indicate a favorable 'time'.

The Prophet (*pbuh*) also said:

No people sit to remember Allah unless the angels encompass them, and the All-Merciful surrounds them, and peace descends upon them, and Allah will remember them.

Special Places

No doubt physical locations and places have their special influence, energy field and chemistry, which affect the power and efficiency of calling and, therefore, the result and effect. On places that have special merit the Prophet (*pbuh*) said, *'Supplications are acceptable when made at the side of the* Ka`bah, *the House of God in Makkah.'* There is also great merit in supplication made in the *Masjid Al-Haram* in Makkah and the Mosque of the Prophet (*pbuh*) in Madinah. Also the Prophet (*pbuh*) has said *'There is great merit in worshiping inside Allah's house, at* Zamzam *and* Safa *and* Marwa *and behind* Maqam Ibrahim, `Arafat, Muzdalifah, Mina *and at the three places where the stoning is done.'* All of those sites are in Makkah or nearby and are stages of the pilgrimage.

There are, of course, many other places on earth that help to increase the power of calling and enhance the state of the caller. Jerusalem, special shrines and places of lesser pilgrimage, and special mosques are among them. Places where prophets, *imam*s and enlightened beings are buried also have a special influence in helping the caller to be better attuned, prepared, focused and in a humble and pleading mode.

When Supplication is Answered

Allah says in the Qur'an:
I will certainly answer the desperate when he calls.

The Prophet (*pbuh*) has said that:

He who has been treated unjustly will be answered even though an unbeliever.

The prayers of a father for his offspring will be answered, prayers of a just spiritual leader (*imam*), prayers of a virtuous man, of a virtuous son, the prayers of the traveler, and for a Muslim brother or sister when not present.

The fastest supplication to be answered is the

calling of a stranger for a stranger.

He who is calling knows his own state of serious need, desperation and urgency. He also knows the extent of his exclusive reliance on Allah. Among the signs that a supplication will be answered is the degree of faith, fearful awareness, a humble heart, weeping and a sense of last resort and desperation. It is also a good sign when the caller feels a relief and lightness as a result of supplication and prayer to Allah.

> The Prophet (*pbuh*) has said:
>
> Actions are as good as their final outcome. Do not judge a person until you see how he seals his action, for it can be that a person acts virtuously only a short time before his death and that causes him to enter the Garden.
>
> Also a person can act evil and die upon this action and that will be the cause for him being in the Fire.

If Allah intends well for His slave He will put him to act virtuously before his death. Thus actions are as good as their final outcome.

Ultimately victory for a believer comes when he is constantly aware of his self and its limitations and weaknesses, and thus recognizes Allah's glorious generosity and ever-present mercy which cover and overcome human frailty and needs. The knowledge of Allah is the key to success in worship and in living one's religion, in preparation for the departure from this world of uncertainty and change, and for the return to the eternal Garden of bliss and its perfection.

Calling

To call upon Allah in times of need and to remember Allah in times of ease are part of the religion of Islam and the cornerstone of worship.

Allah says in the Qur'an:

And whosoever is in taqwā of Allah, He will give him a way out, and will provide for him from where he does not expect it.
And He provides for him from (sources) he never could imagine.
If anyone puts his trust in Allah, sufficient is Allah for him. For Allah will surely accomplish His purpose.
Verily, for all things has Allah appointed a due proportion (measure).
(65:3)

Thus cautious awareness, trust, and reliance upon Allah are the foundation of successful supplication and calling.

Prayers and supplications are motivated by various desires or needs and there are numerous types or levels of calling. One category is to do with unity, praise, and celebration, such as "Oh Lord to you belongs the Praise" (*Rabbanā laka'l-hamd*). A second type is asking for forgiveness and the covering of faults and evil actions, such as, "Oh Allah forgive me" (*Allāhumma ighfirlī*), and "I seek forgiveness of Allah" (*Astaghfirullāh*). Asking for forgiveness is actually asking Allah to 'cover' faults and shortcomings. Returning to the path is conditional upon regret for wrongdoing combined with the determination and commitment to not repeat the same error. A third type, which is the most prevalent, is asking Allah for a removal of an affliction or to bring about the fulfillment of a desire or need, such as, "Oh Allah bring me healing" (*Allāhumma ishfinī*), or, "Oh Allah provide for me" (*Allāhumma ishfinī*), or "Oh Allah give me help or victory" (*Allāhumma unsurnī*).

The courtesy of calling begins with real need and true reliance on Allah exclusively. He is the source and power behind all existence, experience and states.

Allah has revealed to the Prophet (*pbuh*),

I am as good as My slave's expectation of Me.

Expect therefore to be fully answered in the way that Allah knows best and according to His time and grace.

We must also remember what Allah says in the Qur'an:

...You may dislike a thing which is good for you and you may love a thing that is harmful for you. But Allah knows and you know not.

(2:216)

Courtesies of Supplication

The courtesies of the caller include physical cleanliness, to be ritually pure, to face the direction of prayer (*qiblah*), to lift one's hands, to start by saying, "In the Name of Allah," (*bismillāh*), to praise the Prophet (*pbuh*), and to have the mind focused upon Allah, His greatness, generosity and mercy. To have one's heart present, humbly, but in high anticipation and positiveness.

Every situation has its special supplication: e.g. before eating, whilst eating, after eating, when waking up, before sleeping, before leaving the house, before entering the bathroom and so on.

The Prophet (*pbuh*) has said:

He who has needs, let him be on good ablution (*wudu'*), and pray two cycles, and then praise Allah and send blessings upon the Prophet (*pbuh*) and his family, and then make his supplication.

It is most important to be in certainty that Allah hears and that He will answer, yet repeatedly call often, and relentlessly.

As already mentioned, it is important to choose the appropriate time for supplication, as well as places that are conducive. The fasting month of Ramadan and the Night of Power, the month of Sha`ban, the first ten days of the month of Muharram (*'Āshūrā'*) and many other days are known to have special qualities. Pre-dawn supplication, before breaking fast, and in the afternoon are preferred times. As for places, Makkah, Madinah, and numerous holy sites have greater benefits.

Allah says:

O My servants who have transgressed against their souls! Despair not of the Mercy of Allah, for Allah forgives all sins; for He is Often Forgiving, Most Merciful.
(39:53)

The Prophet (*pbuh*) has said:

Allah answers the call of a sincere Muslim in one of three ways: either He will give what is asked for, or He will save it for the Hereafter, or He will ward off an equivalent evil from him.

If one has made supplication and not received evidence of an answer, then one must return with stronger faith and trust and call again and again. When one calls upon Allah for worldly provision and property one must equally strive in the world looking for appropriate opportunity and openings.

> *That (the fruit of) his striving will soon come in sight. (53:40)*
> *And anyone who has done an atom's weight of good, shall see it!*
> *(99:7)*

The believer trusts that Allah knows and desires the best for us at all times. Thus he delegates his needs and future to Allah's Will whilst striving for the best. In this quest the believer emulates the Prophetic model in action, thought and state. Muhammad (*pbuh*) exemplified the perfect universal being. He was the Qur'an, the discerner between falsehood and truth and the religion itself, walking on earth. There is nothing better for us in this world than to attain knowledge and awareness of Allah's ever-presence, mercy and love and that He knows what is best for us and will give us that which is appropriate and deserved, for He is the All-Just.

Supplication of Allah's Names and Attributes

Allah's mercy is wider and greater than we think. Yet in our earthly state, our needs can be diverse and specific. Thus, we are in constant need to alleviate pain or harm, or to bring about the desired goodness. Calling upon His Names and Attributes is a means of acknowledging our weakness of and turning to the desirable quality of the Name or Attribute so as to submerge ourselves fully in the quality called upon.

As the most desirable qualities in this life are those ascribed to the Creator, we human beings wish to acquire aspects of these qualities to varying degrees, according to the circumstances we are in. There are, however, general tendencies in the human state that cause some of us to become more connected with a particular attribute. Connection with a particular attribute usually comes about because of the special quality of that attribute, or to complement states or conditions in the person's character.

Throughout the Muslim world it has become a custom when a child is born to ask a learned man or sage to name the child. With insight and inspiration the name will reflect the natural tendency, future orientation, or need of the child. It is hoped that by attaching a Divine Attribute to the name of the child it will become his or her dominant trait. As an example: `Abd al-Rahmān (Servant of the All-Merciful) is given to a child to enhance tendencies of clemency and tenderness, or to a child who possesses a very benign and generous disposition. `Abd al-Hakim (servant of the most Wise), may be given to a child who clearly shows the potential for wisdom and knowledge, or in the hope that this quality will be reflected in his life. Most Muslim communities live, invoke and interact with constant reference to Allah and His Attributes to which they aspire. In this way, it can be seen that Muslim societies are constantly performing collective supplication.

In conclusion all human needs and shortcomings which lead to supplication are none other than part of Allah's subtle mercy to bring His creation's attention and awareness back to Him. Allah declared that He was a hidden treasure and He loved to be known and thus He created. Our needs are part of His design to be known and the ultimate purpose of supplication and calling is to express our weakness and dependence on Him. Our actions are only part of the worship of Him; while His gifts and mercy are aspects of His love, grace and generosity, and their occasional coincidence is part of His wisdom.

The awakened person of excellence sees in supplication the opportunity to call upon the true Beloved and is not veiled from the source, when rejoicing as the fruits of his calling manifest themselves. He who knows the self knows His Lord and loves Him with unconditional passion and dedication.

THE END – WITH ENDLESS BEGINNINGS

Human needs, intentions and actions are based on the two main motivating forces within us: to attract what is desirable and repel what is undesirable. However, the primal essential power behind all movement as designed by Allah is to lead us back to the root and cause of all existence: Allah Himself. It is through faith, cautious awareness and self-knowledge that we begin to ascend the ladder of unity back to the source from where we originated. In reality, it is where we already are, but without full awareness of the magnitude of the present.

Supplication, prayer and, indeed, all forms of worship, praise of Allah and other rituals and practices, formal or spontaneous, are all signs of the yearning to return to the sanctum and lasting security of the Creator. Supplication is the handy spiritual rope which connects the seeker with the sought.

Supplication began with the first of all human beings, our father Adam, when he admitted his mistake and asked forgiveness, that is to be covered by Allah's mercy and forbearance. Adam's natural disposition was pure and had no exposure to deceit until the affliction of the devil, or the lower negative tendencies (*shaytān*) occurred.

In Islam we have a very rich culture of great examples of supplication from the prophets and messengers, mentioned in the Qur'an and historical records. Our great

Prophet Ebrahim (*pbuh*) asked:

> *Fill some hearts among men with love towards them,*
> *and provide them with fruits,*
> *so that they may give thanks.*
> *(14:37)*

The Prophet Muhammad (*pbuh*) has said:

Supplication is the weapon of the believer, the pillār of the religion, and the lights of the heavens and the earth.

From him and his family and companions, we have a great selection of supplications for different occasions. A selection of supplications can be found in Part III.

The Way Supplication Works

All human beings were created with the potential of manifesting a degree of a Divine Attribute, as these divine traits are latent in our inherent nature (*fitrah*). All of the attributes manifest to a greater or lesser degree according to the preparedness and orientation of the individual. The way supplication and prayer work is that the caller is prepared and in tune to receiving the appropriate opening and quality of an attribute through the act of calling on and pleading for an answer. The more desperate and in need one is when calling upon Allah with sincerity and expectation, the more likely one is to connect with the desirable attribute and answer.

All of the Divine Attributes or Names are like heavenly rivers or shafts of light, connecting the physical and material realities with the unseen. Therefore, when the believer addresses any of the Attributes with complete dedication and sincerity, it is like opening the doors connecting our world to the Originator of patterns in the realm of the unseen. Then these energy patterns of Attributes reverberate in the self and enhance that desirable state within the heart, and manifest the outcome.

For example, if one is feeling weak or vulnerable and seeking strength, calling upon *Al-Qawī* (The most Strong) will bring about an inner resonance of personal power. The Qur'an describes this process as taking on the 'color' of Allah (*sibghat Allāh*).

> *(We take our) color from Allah – And what coloring could be better than Allah's?*
> *It is Him (alone) we worship.*
> *(2:138)*

Similarly, affliction or sickness is a divine call to manifest the cosmic power of healing by being a channel for it. Therefore, every experience in this existence is divinely blessed for it is by difficulty that we experience mercy and ease.

In truth, divine mercy encompasses every known or unknown entity in existence. Allah's is the eternal power and light and the self longs to manifest His Attributes as best as it can, according to its capability. He is the perfect ever-present Source that everyone longs for and is in passionate love with.

PART II
DIVINE PERFECTION

INTRODUCTION

Over the past dozen centuries several popular lists of Divine Names have been circulating among Muslims. Most of these lists have their origin in Prophetic tradition, which tells us that to Allah belong 99 Names, and whoever has recited them, that is, whoever knows and calls upon them, will enter the Garden.

As mentioned earlier, the list of Names attributed to the Prophet (*pbuh*) varies according to different sources. Indeed, there are some traditions which list several hundred Names or Attributes of Allah. The list most widely distributed among Muslims during the past decades has probably its origin in Imam Abu Hamid Al-Ghazali's book (11th century CE) entitled, *Al-Maqsad Al-Asna*.

In the Qur'an, however, there are 127 Names that are directly attributable to Allah and many more which are inferred: for example *tawfiq* (success or enablement), the noun of which would be *Muwaffiq* (one who grants Success or Enables). The word *tawfiq*, appears in the Qur'an (11:88), but not the noun form. There are also a number of Names that are referred to in the Qur'an which are compound Names and not often used in supplication, such as Dhū al-Intiqām (Possessor of Retribution), Dhū al-'Arsh (Possessor of the Throne), Rāfi' al-Darajāt (Possessor of Exalted Ranks), Khayr al-Wārithīn (The Best of Inheritors), and others. The list of compound names is found at the end of Part II.

Some Names relate only to Allah's essence, such as Allah, Al-Quddūs (The Most Pure), Al-`Azīz (The All-Mighty), Al-`Adhīm (The Magnificent), Al-Kabīr (The Incomparably Great), Al-Jalīl (The Majestic), Al-Haqq (The Absolute truth), Al-Hayy (The Ever-Living), Al-Wāhid (The One), Al-Ahad (The Absolute One), Al-Samad (The Self-Sufficient), Al-Muta`āli (The Most Exalted), Al-Nūr (The Light), Al-Fard (The Unique One) and Al-Witr (The Singular).

Some Names relate to Allah's majesty (*Jalāl*), in that these Names represent the active or masculine attribute in existence. According to Islamic cosmology, all existence is based upon a harmonious polarity of the active or masculine (*Jalāl*) and receptive or feminine (*Jamāl*) attributes. The Divine Names of Majesty are: Al-Jabbār (The Compeller), Al-Mutakabbir (The Supremely Great), Al-Qahhār (The Subduer), Al-Qābid (The Restrictor), Al-Khāfid (The Debaser), Al-Mudhill (The Abaser), Al-Raqīb (The All-Vigilant), Al-Wāsi` (The Vast), Al-Mājid (The Most Glorious), Al-Qawī (The Most Strong), Al-Matīn (The Firm), Al-Muīd (The Returner), Al-Mūmīt (The Death Giver), Al-Mānī` (The Preventer), Al-Dārr (The Bestower of Affliction), Al-Wārith (The Inheritor), Al-Sabūr (The Patient) and Al-Shahid (The All-Witnessing).

Other Divine Names relate to His Beauty (*Jamāl*), which are the receptive or female attributes in existence: Al-Rahīm (The All-Compassionate), Al-Salām (The Bestower of Peace), Al-Mu'min (The Trustworthy), Al-Musawwir (The Fashioner), Al-Ghafūr (The All-Forgiving), Al-Razzāq (The Ever-Providing), Al-Fattāh (The Opener), Al-Bāsit (The Expander), Al-Latīf (The Subtle), Al-Halīm (The Clement), Al-Karīm (The Most Generous), Al-`Afūw (The

Pardoner), Al-Ra'ūf (The Most Affectionate), Al-Mughnī (The Enricher), Al-Nāfi` (The Bestower of Benefit), Al-Hādi (The Guide), Al-Jamīl (The Beautiful) and Al-Qarīb (The Near One).

Seven Divine Names are often referred to as the Key Names or Attributes in that most other names are derived from them: Al-Hayy (The Ever-Living), Al-Qādir (The Most Able), Al-Murīd (He Who wills), Al-`Alīm (The All-Knowing), Al-Samī` (The All-Hearing), Al-Basīr (The All-Seeing) and Al-Mutakallim (The Communicator). All of these Attributes belong to the One Creator Who has bestowed aspects of them on His created beings and we experience these Attributes in a limited and specific way.

All Divine Names and Attributes are like facets of one divine cosmic principle. The all-encompassing Name of this essence is Allah, and every facet reflects its own special color and relates to other attributes closest to it.

We have also mentioned how each Name or Attribute can be used as invocation to restore the soul to proper balance. For example, when one is sick the appropriate Attribute to call upon is the Healer (*Al-Shāfī*). When one is in a state of agitation, calling upon *Al-Salām* (The Bestower of Peace) will bring tranquility and wholesomeness of heart.

Creation is at all times under the control of Allah, the All-Mighty, All-Merciful and Ever-Present. Allah draws us close to Him through our needs and inadequacies so that we come to realize His perfection and absoluteness. The seeker's appropriate response would be to call upon the desired name or attribute that will take him or her close to the divine source from which all other attributes emanate and engulf creation.

Allah states in the Qur'an that the purpose of creation

is to worship Him. We can only worship what we adore and know, so knowledge of Him is given to us through the doors and windows of His attributes.

Calling upon these names and attributes in invocation is a means of submitting to the One Who encompasses all. The final station of this process is the firm establishment of a transformative knowledge, which renders the seeker totally aware, that at all times there is none other than Him. As creation we have shortcomings which drive us towards the realization of the Perfect. Indeed, our imperfection is the key to the realization of the Perfect Lord.

A Divine Name is only an indication and a mirror that reflects the One Reality, Allah, (glory be to Him), and the Name is not the same as the reality. It is said that whoever worships the Name and not the reality is in denial of the One true Reality, while whoever worships the Name and its meaning is worshipping other-than-Allah, whereas, whoever worships the meaning and not its Name is in true unity.

THE ETERNAL QUEST

As mentioned before, all human beings show a constant drive or desire towards a state or condition, which we call knowledge of truth. This truth (*Haqq*) is called Allah.

Thus Allah is the ultimate goal towards which all intentions and actions move. Allah is also the source that caused the initial drive and energy for it in the first place. That same source is also the cause of maintaining that drive. Thus we can say that Allah's purpose and Will is simply that of divine effulgence, and its realization is creation: all of which is totally dependent on Him, at all times and in all circumstances. This is why the enlightened ones realize that His Will is done and evident for all who can see.

Allah describes Himself in the Qur'an as the eternal, unique and all-encompassing Light. From that original pure Light emanate infinite varieties of creational entities energized by that Light and the modifications of it. Thus from a pure unity point of view one can say there is only Light. Equally, we must admit experientially the worldly and manifested domain of duality and change, and the cosmology of time and space. All of these realities are shadows or 'overflows' of Light.

The prophets, messengers and enlightened beings in every past culture and nation have all echoed the truth of the One behind, within, before and after what appears as diverse manifestations. He is the source of life and we as creation do experience life. He is the source and cause of ability, and we do experience and possess some ability for a while. The same partial sharing or manifestation applies to many of the Divine Names and Attributes.

The means to clear understanding of this most crucial and mysterious issue has also been disclosed in the sacred books and the way of the prophets. The path of unity begins where we are by admitting human shortcomings, weaknesses, and needs; and this admittance and submission will lead us to reaching the perfect model and way of beingness to which we aspire. Thus, a living faith and belief begin to illumine our path from Allah to Allah and by Allah. The state of excellence is essentially that of pure awareness. From that awakened state we can observe and correct all other lesser states, or tarnished and confused conditions. The original Light from within will illumine all changing shadows around us.

The application of surrender (*islām*), faith (*īmān*) and excellence (*ihsān*) is achieved by adherence to the code of conduct (*sharī`ah*) and self-knowledge. To empty and purify the self and groom it, gives rise to the virtues of courage and modesty, from which comes wisdom. These traits within the self bring about a reference to the source of truth and justice and will lead to witnessing His light. Thus, the virtues of courage, modesty, wisdom and justice are the foundation upon which the enlightened self emerges in illumined worship and divine passion.

The self is now in a true state of adoration and worship of Allah, for it sees the divine qualities and attributes in every manifestation and experience. Thus one who is in this state is called a universal being (*Insān al-Kāmil*). All human beings knowingly or unknowingly aspire to this state. Allah has created only to be worshipped and this cannot occur fully unless He is witnessed at all times.

Allah's Attributes, Names and qualities are thus the beams of Light that we seek as we journey through this life. His Names are indications of His presence and powers to be relied upon and drawn close to.

THE DIVINE NAMES

As mentioned earlier Allah's essence and original Light radiate and overflow into all realms of creation. Anything that exists, appears, or lives, has within it an aspect of this light energy, and thus it is in Allah's kingdom.

We, as the Adamic tribe, have within our innate nature (*fitrah*) a yearning and love for all the primal streams and shafts of lights, which have the beautiful and desirable qualities of Allah. These Attributes are referred to in the Qur'an and in the Prophetic teachings as the Most Beautiful or Glorious Names. Most of these Attributes are universally acknowledged as great virtues or high qualities. Indeed, sages, saints and great leaders often show some of these traits and qualities.

The human task is to relate and connect to the appropriate quality or Name and be engulfed and absorbed by its glorious quality to realize its immediately present reality. Each and every quality meets all of the other Attributes in the all-encompassing One. This great mystery can never be resolved. It will dissolve and yield its truth, when we ourselves submit and die into its truth. It is the death of the individual identity that will reveal His supreme presence.

Allah's eternal presence and manifestation through His Glorious Attributes have been there from before creation and will continue after the end of all creation. Our responsibility is to yield and submit to His signs through our needs, shortcomings and other dependencies. He has created us such that we submit, read the signs, and follow with faith and confidence in His Grace. All of His names, signs, attributes and qualities are signposts along His path. We are led by Him unto Him.

TRADITION AND HISTORY OF THE POPULAR LIST OF 99 NAMES

As mentioned earlier a tradition from the Prophet (*pbuh*) states that to Allah belong 99 Names and whoever recites or enumerates them will enter the Garden.

Gratitude and contentment at heart are what 'tether' and increase Allah's gifts, both subtle and material; while patience and constancy in cautious awareness repels distractions and other pitfalls.

As we earlier noted, there are certain variations in the lists of 99 Names as handed down and recorded by the different Islamic sources, foremost among them al-Tirmidhi and al-Ghazali. For example, the Names mentioned by Hakim contain twenty-eight Names that are not mentioned by Ibn Majah. There are also differences in the Names and Attributes handed down through the school of the Prophetic household.

However, more important than defining exactly or exclusively the 99 Names referred to by the Prophet (*pbuh*), is to come to know and connect with the actual meaning and quality of the Divine Names and Attributes. The Prophetic tradition regarding Allah's Names was not meant to restrict them to 99. In our list we include Allah and *Al-Rabb* (The Lord), thus reaching 101 Names. What matters most is the understanding and focus upon the appropriate door of Allah, and the courteous approach and calling upon that Attribute.

The Divine Attributes and Names are of different levels. At the highest they are exclusively sacred, while at the creational level they relate to actions such as the Creator and the Most Able. At another level the Names relate to a quality or meaning such as the All-Forgiving, the All-Knowing and so on.

There is another category of Names involving action, such as Al-Mu'min, which means the Trustworthy, and also the Confirmer of Truth, as well as the Giver of Faith. Al-Rabb means the Lord or Master, Authority and Commander. Al-Rabb brings up Creation to its full potential.

There are, however, some desirable qualities that cannot be attributed to Allah such as courage, steadfastness and modesty. Similarly, some attributes relate only to creation, such as weakness, ignorance, impoverishment, and death.

Irrespective of which sphere the Divine Attributes belong to, they are all like heavenly rivers, or shafts of light, connecting the physical and material realities with the unseen, subtle angelic powers, and other energies and lights. Therefore when the *mu'min* addresses any of these Attributes with total dedication and sincerity, it is like opening doors connecting our world to the Originator of Patterns in the realm of the unseen. Then these great patterns of Attributes reverberate in the mirror of our self and enhance that desirable energy within the heart. It is the transformation and new light that we seek on the path of spiritual progress.

In truth, Divine Names are none other than divine presences appropriate within the nature and potential of all existence. Everything in this universe contains its primal pattern, (*fitrah*), which reflects the truth. Thus divine qualities encompassing essence, attribute and action are recognized within the intellect (`aql*) and heart of the disciplined believer who has subdued the self.

EXPLORING HIS DOMINION

We as created beings are programmed to seek knowledge, truth and certainty. Everything we experience in life is transient and the end is uncertain. Yet, we always aspire for perfect beauty and majesty.

Reflecting upon Allah's Attributes and qualities reveals channels and highways leading to His courtyard. Any situation we are in has a reality which leads us closer to the truth, if we seek that from Him.

Indeed, He is closer to us than our jugular vein.

All of life and its experiences are acts of worship for the sincere seeker, and the Beautiful Names are energizers of the self on its journey to reality. Allah alone is the Real, the Originator, and only He is everlasting; and to Him all return. Why then are we veiled from this freedom? The remedy lies in surrender (*islām*), faith (*īmān*) and excellence (*ihsān*), and living in the eternal messages of 'There is no God, but Allah, and Muhammad is his Prophet.' *Lā ilāha il Allah, Muhammadun Rasūl Allah.*

ALLAH'S BEAUTIFUL NAMES AND ATTRIBUTES

1. ALLĀH
2. AL-RAHMĀN – The All-Merciful
3. AL-RAHĪM – The All-Compassionate
4. AL-MALIK – The King
5. AL-QUDDŪS – The Most Pure
6. AL-SALĀM – The Bestower of Peace
7. AL-MU'MIN – The Trustworthy
8. AL-MUHAYMIN – The Safeguarder
9. AL-`AZĪZ – The All-Mighty
10. AL-JABBĀR – The Compeller
11. AL-MUTAKABBIR – The Supremely Great
12. AL-KHĀLIQ – The Creator
13. AL-BĀRI' – The Maker
14. AL-MUSAWWIR – The Fashioner
15. AL-GHAFFĀR – The Coverer of all Faults
16. AL-QAHHĀR – The Subduer
17. AL-WAHHĀB – The Bestower
18. AL-RAZZĀQ – The Ever-Providing
19. AL-FATTĀH – The Opener
20. AL-`ALĪM – The All-Knowing
21. AL-QĀBID – The Restrictor
22. AL-BĀSIT – The Expander
23. AL-KHĀFID – The Debaser
24. AL-RĀFI` – The Exalter

25. AL-MU`IZZ – The Honorer
26. AL-MUDHILL – The Abaser
27. AL-SAMĪ` – The All-Hearing
28. AL-BASĪR – The All-Seeing
29. AL-HAKAM – The Judge
30. AL-`ADL – The All-Just
31. AL-LATĪF – The Subtle
32. AL-KHABĪR – The All-Cognizant
33. AL-HALĪM – The Clement
34. AL-`ADHĪM – The Magnificent
35. AL-GHAFŪR – The All-Forgiving
36. AL-SHAKŪR – The Grateful
37. AL-`ALĪ – The Most High
38. AL-KABĪR – The Incomprehensibly Great
39. AL-HAFIDH – The Preserver
40. AL-MUQĪT – The Sustainer
41. AL-HASĪB – The Reckoner
42. AL-JALĪL – The Majestic
43. AL-KARĪM – The Most Generous
44. AL-RAQĪB – The All-Vigilant
45. AL-MUJĪB – The Responder
46. AL-WĀSI` – The Vast
47. AL-HAKĪM – The Most Wise
48. AL-WADŪD – The All-Loving
49. AL-MAJĪD – The Most Glorious
50. AL-BĀ`ITH – The Resurrector
51. AL-SHAHĪD – The All-Witnessing
52. AL-HAQQ – The Absolute Truth
53. AL-WAKĪL – The Guardian Trustee
54. AL-QAWĪ – The Most Strong
55. AL-MATĪN – The Firm
56. AL-WALĪ – The Patron
57. AL-HAMĪD – The Praiseworthy

58. AL-MUHSI – The Appraiser
59. AL-MUBDĪ` – The Originator
60. AL-MU`ĪD – The Returner
61. AL-MUHYĪ – The Life-Giver
62. AL-MUMĪT – The Death-Giver
63. AL-HAYY – The Ever-Living
64. AL-QAYYŪM – The All-Sustaining
65. AL-WĀJID – The Manifestor
66. Al-Mājid – The Most Splendid
67. AL-WĀHID – The One
68. AL-AHAD – The Absolute One
69. AL-SAMAD – The Self-Sufficient
70. AL-QĀDIR – The Most Able
71. AL-MUQTADIR – The All-Powerful
72. AL-MUQADDIM – The Expediter
73. AL-MU'AKHKHIR – The Postponer
74. AL-AWWAL – The First
75. AL-ĀKHIR – The Last
76. AL-DHĀHIR – The Manifest
77. AL-BĀTIN – The Concealed
78. AL-WALĪ – The Governor
79. AL-MUTA`ĀLĪ – The Most Exalted
80. AL-BARR – The Benefactor
81. AL-TAWWAB – The Most Accepting of Repentance
82. AL-MUNTAQIM – He who brings about Trial and Affliction
83. AL-`AFŪW – The Pardoner
84. AL-RA'ŪF – The Most Affectionate
85. MĀLIK AL-MULK – The Master of The Kingdom
86. DHŪ AL-JALĀLI WA AL-IKRĀM – The Master of Majesty and Nobility
87. AL-MUQSIT – The All-Equitable
88. AL-JĀMI` – The Gatherer

89. AL-GHANI – The Rich Beyond Need
90. AL-MUGHNI – The Enricher
91. AL-MĀNI` – The Preventer
92. AL-DĀRR – The Bestower of Affliction
93. AL-NĀFI` – The Bestower of Benefit
94. AL-NŪR – The Light
95. AL-HĀDI – The Guide
96. AL-BADĪ` – The Innovator
97. AL-BĀQI – The Everlasting
98. AL-WĀRITH – The Inheritor
99. AL-RASHĪD – The Most Discerning
100. AL-SABŪR – The Patient
101. AL-RABB – The Lord

ALLĀH

Ilāh means god, *al-Ilāh* means 'the God'. Allah designates the Source from which all things seen and unseen emanate and to which they return.

Allah is a proper noun indicating the essence, *dhāt*, from which all attributes and names emanate. Allah is the self-effulgent and all-Encompassing Source of all creation in the heavens and on earth. Allah's power is all-evident and yet He is not seen or definable. Allah is beyond comparison, most unique, all-encompassing, ever-present, Light of lights.

Allah is the ultimate and most powerful Name to call upon. One can call upon Allah and then call upon any desirable attribute (or vice versa), thereby invoking the root of all attributes – Allah.

AL-RAHMĀN
The All-Merciful

From the root *rahima* the following meanings are derived: to be merciful; to have mercy upon; *rahim* means womb or kinship; *arhām* (plural of *rahīm*) means blood relative. The two names Al-Rahmān and Al-Rahīm are often found together and thus intensify each other. Dhūl-Rahmah, 'Possessor of Mercy,' is also a Divine Name from the same root. Allah's mercy and blessings are constantly showered upon all creation at all times, although most of creation does not experience it, because they are veiled by darkness and grossness of self concern. Al-Rahmān's lights of mercy encompass the entire cosmos. In the Qur'an it is connected with *Bismi'llah* (In the Name of Allah) and is repeated 114 times, which is the number of chapters (*suras*) although one *sura* starts without it, implying that mercy is the first Attribute of Allah which covers all times and circumstances. His mercy (*rahmah*) permeates all existence and experiences and when the believer calls upon this great Attribute with courtesy and faith, he will discover its vast effect on all situations and states. Calling on *Al-Rahmān* could lead to Al-`Alīm, knowledge and understanding of your situation.

AL-RAHIM
The All-Compassionate

The root of Al-Rahīm is the same as Al-Rahmān, but whereas *Rahmān* is general and applies to all existence, *Rahīm* is specific and conditional. Sickness is part of the gifts of Al-Rahmān, whereas seeking healing and remedy is the domain of Al-Rahīm. The relationship of Al-Rahīm to Al-Rahmān is like the eye to the full human body. One is particular and special, whilst the other is all-encompassing. When need is identified and is clearly important to you personally, it is then that the energy of Al-Rahīm needs to be absorbed by the caller.

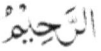

AL-MALIK
The King

From the root *malaka*: to possess or to own; to have power over (someone or something) exclusively; to dominate. The following words are also derivatives: *mulk*, dominion, sovereignty, right of possession; *malik*, king, monarch. *Mulk* is the realm of the physical manifestation created by Allah, while *malakūt* is the realm of sovereignty.

As the owner and ruler of all creation, the Creator's power is all-evident as the Al-Malik who manages the affairs of His creation with justice and perfection at all times. All cosmic realities are subjects in the realm of the mighty King of all known and unknown entities.

In the presence of the Al-Malik, you may gain access to His powers. You may also be shown levels of His kingship and sovereignty, for all belongs to Him acknowledging in truth that He is the only King. When you receive a most beautiful gift, He is the owner and you are the one who is loaned. To acknowledge the loan, you must constantly acknowledge the one to whom all things are subject, for in truth, He is the only King.

AL-QUDDŪS
The Most Pure

From the root *qaddasa*; to sanctify or consecrate; and *qadasa*, to be pure; *quddūs*, most holy; *qudsī*, holy, sacred.

Absolute purity and freedom from all defects is the Attribute of Al-Quddūs. The entire creation is engulfed by the holy, sacred and sublime web of Al-Quddūs.

This Attribute is often combined with other attributes to show that absolute sanctity is also connected with power and kingship, or other qualities. He owns everything, and all creation is in His treasury, yet He is not tarnished or affected by His kingship.

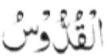

AL-SALĀM
The Bestower of Peace

From the root *salama*; to be safe and sound. Also, (*salam*), peace; *sallama*, to preserve, surrender, greet or salute; *aslama*, to abandon, surrender, commit oneself to the will of Allah. The words, Islam and Muslim, come from this verbal form; *taslīm* means either surrender or salutation; *Dar al-Salām* means the abode of peace, or Paradise.

Allah is the door to inner tranquility, ease, peace, and contentment. There can be no discontent when there is peace of mind and heart, and it implies wholesomeness and being free from any fault. *Salām* and *amn* (safety, peace, security) relate to freedom from harm, fear and defect.

The divine precinct of peace, pure bliss and perfection is without any ripple of disturbance. It is a perfect attribute of the Garden to which we all yearn to return. It is the state of the heart of the prophets and enlightened ones.

AL-MU'MIN
The Trustworthy

From the root *amina* or *amuna*, meaning to be secure; to be faithful; to trust; the following are derived: *āmana*, to believe; *īmān*, faith, belief, being true to the trust Allah has bestowed on one by firm belief in the heart, not just the tongue. A *mu'min* is one who believes that he is subject to divine security and promise. The name Al-Amīn, meaning trustworthy, loyal, honest, is how the Prophet Muhammad (*pbuh*) was described.

Allah is the source of *īmān* and all that which emanates from this Divine Attribute. We call to Al-Mu'min for protection, comfort and trust, for He is Ever-Present.

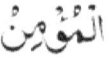

AL-MUHAYMIN
The Safeguarder

From the root *haymana*: to protect and preserve, regulate, control – hence to safeguard. *Haymanah* means extreme and total watchfulness and protection.

Allah watches over, protects and controls all things, and He always has the control and power of His decrees. He is the monitor, witnesser and judge of His creation according to His perfect plan. He bestows what is needed for His realization.

The remembrance of the real protector and absolute dominator will always bring about relief and ease for the sincere seeker who is always looking for the One.

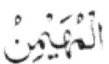

AL-'AZĪZ
The All-Mighty

From the root `azza; to be rare, precious, scarce, to become dear; to become powerful, strong; `azzaza, to make strong, fortify; to know; to exalt.

Allah is the pure Light behind all manifesting lights and existences. He is most subtle, beyond comprehension, definition or delineation and therefore He is sublimely precious, dear and unique. Al-'Azīz means the unique in glory who will always prevail. The more the seeker experiences humility, abasement, and self-effacement, the more he will realize Allah's `izzah, or might and glory.

To relate to the true Source of everlasting might, call and contemplate the One `Aziz.

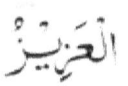

AL-JABBĀR
The Compeller

From the root *jabara*: to set; to restore to a good state; to compel. *Jabbār* means powerful, forceful, compelling.

All existences follow simple and natural laws and decrees toward a destiny. Allah compels all situations to flow towards the original Will and purpose for which He had them created. He propels all creation according to His will. His ultimate purpose for creation is submission, acknowledgement, and thus worship of Himself.

Human injustice, despotism and tyranny are balanced by Allah's perfect justice, compulsion and power, in this world and in the Hereafter.

AL-MUTAKABBIR
The Supremely Great

From *takabbara*, to be proud, which derives from *kabara*: to be older than another in estimation of rank or dignity; to be great; to grow. *Kabbara* means to glorify or exalt Allah, by saying 'Allahu Akbar' (known as the *takbīr*). Allah is greater than whatever can be encompassed by any human comprehension, understanding or vision.

Al-Mutakabbir is an Attribute of the One Who has brought everything into existence, by Himself, through His own power. Allah's greatness is matched by His condescension to create Adam and all short-lived creation. Thus He is worthy of pride. We take refuge in Al-Mutakabbir from human pretension and arrogance.

Human arrogance, vanity and haughtiness are balanced and overcome by Allah's everlasting greatness and glory.

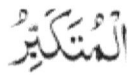

AL-KHĀLIQ
The Creator

From the root *khalaqa*: to create, originate; to mould or form. To bring into being entities from non-existence is the work of Al-Khāliq. He manifests and brings forth universes and spheres of creation, subtle and gross – all relating and unified in His Light. Everything that is created has an outer appearance, meaning, and finite potential and an end of its form in the physical world.

To call upon Al-Khāliq is to wonder about the infinite array of creational manifestation and to contemplate the intricate balance and interdependence of creation, seen and unseen.

AL-BĀRI'
The Maker

From the root *bara'a*: to create or make – usually used in reference to Allah only; *barīyah* is creation.

Allah has created the cosmos and all existence from non-existence. Thus the whole universe was raised from the original void and its apparent solidity is based on 'modified' light and its qualities. It is the most original and unique act of glory by the One Maker to have made things impossible possible.

To call upon Al-Bāri' is to contemplate the subtler creational attributes, the magic of bringing forth from the unseen – the divine magic.

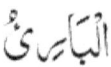

AL-MUSAWWIR
The Fashioner

From *sawwara*: to form or to fashion a thing; to render an image; also to imagine or conceive of something.

The subtle original Light radiates beams of light, angels, and spirits, giving rise to shapes and manifestations. Behind every shape there is a meaning and behind that is the Essence. When one adores a beautiful object, one is seeking beauty behind its actual form. Al-Musawwir has brought about infinite varieties of outer shapes and appearances with equally infinite dynamic relationships.

We often invoke Him when we glorify a facet of creation which we normally could not imagine or perceive.

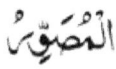

AL-GHAFFĀR
The Coverer of all Faults

From the root *ghafara* the following meanings are derived: to cover, to pardon, to forgive; *ghufrān* is forgiveness, pardon. Allah is described as *Khayr al-Ghāfirīn* in the Qur'an (7:155).

Allah is forever covering, concealing, healing and forgiving. Thus we are given many opportunities to Heighten our awareness, change our intentions and actions, and return to the natural path meant for us: to submit, know and worship Him.

Whenever one has continually made the same errors, call upon Him Who has witnessed them and abandon that habit. Al-Ghaffār forgives multiple recurring errors.

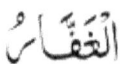

AL-QAHHĀR
The Subduer

From the root *qahara*: to subjugate; to overpower, conquer and predominate. *Qāhir* – the Dominant or the Conqueror, comes from the same root and is another form of this Divine Name (6:18).

Wise human beings recognize their inherent weakness and the absolute power of the Creator. Al-Qahhār overcomes all forms of power, subtle and gross, and all plans and controls. He prevails over His creations and His original scheme will always succeed.

When one is afflicted by injustice or human force, one pleads to the source of dominance: Al-Qahhār.

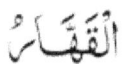

AL-WAHHĀB
The Bestower

From the root verb *wahaba*: to give; to endow; to bestow.

Allah gives unconditionally to all His creation and according to His mercy and knowledge of what is best for them in their progress. The gifts of Allah start with the act of creating existence and experience, leading to the greatest gift of all: increased knowledge of the Ever-Present Creator. One invokes Al-Wahhāb begging for undeserved gifts, from Him Who does not calculate and measure the way we do, for His treasury has no limits or bounds.

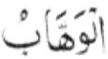

AL-RAZZĀQ
The Ever-Providing

From the root *razaqa*: to supply with the necessities of life, to provide for; to bestow upon; to sustain. *Rizq* is provision, sustenance, or anything from which one benefits in growth, evolvement, ease and peace.

Allah is the source and power behind all provisions for all creatures at all times. Allah provides all needs according to the natural and subtle laws which govern creation. *Rizq* is not always what we think we want. He allocates what is appropriate for creation to yield and fulfill the highest in their potential. The power of Al-Razzāq includes material and subtler provision for mind, body and soul.

One calls upon Al-Razzāq whenever one feels a need or deprivation, at any level, for *rizq* includes all types of provisions needed on this journey.

AL-FATTĀH
The Opener

Fataha is from the root meaning to open; to turn on; to conquer; to reveal; to grant a mercy or victory. *Surat al-Fātihah* opens the Qur'an; *miftāh* is a key. *Khayr al-Fātihīn*: The Best of Openers (7:89).

Allah always opens new horizons and doors, and provides solutions and relief. *Fath* is also an insight into new knowledge and the removal of veils and limitations in life's progress. He removes obstacles and opens His treasury of lights and delights.

During difficulties one calls upon Al-Fattāh who holds the keys for appropriate insights, openings and new horizons of actions and possibilities.

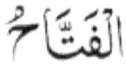

AL-`ALĪM
The All-Knowing

From the root `alima: to know, to become acquainted with; to encompass knowledges concealed; to distinguish. `Ilm is knowledge or science.

Allah is the source of all that is to be known before time, in time and after time. His boundless knowledge is the foundation of lordship and universal supremacy. Absolute knowledge rules over all relative knowledge. He knows best what we intend, the outcome of all actions, and what is most conducive to our real and lasting contentment, based on *īmān* and basking in His secure presence.

In ignorance, confronted with choices and uncertainties, call upon Al-`Alīm and trust and depend upon Him. Knowing little does not matter when we know He Who knows all, and that He will give us what is needed at the appropriate time, and by the means He knows best.

AL-QĀBID
The Restrictor

From the root *qabada*: to contract; to seize, grasp; to constrict and restrict; to control possibilities. Al-Qābid does not appear in the Qur'an as such but appears in its verbal form (2:245).

Allah is the original cause behind experiences of restriction and constriction. All creation is subjected to experiences which relate to the *nafs* or lower self. The *Mu'min* has little to fear when in constriction, because his choices become fewer and therefore mistakes are less likely. Al-Qābid also extracts the *rūh* out of the body at the point of death by means of His angel. Al-Qābid restricts and shields the evil of wrongdoers. This Attribute balances Al-Bāsit, the Expander.

AL-BĀSIT
The Expander

From the root *basata*: to expand, enlarge; to unfold; to spread out; to make wide and ample. Al-Bāsit is expressed in the Qur'an in its verbal form (13:14).

Allah is the source of ease, flow, growth and expansion. All Creation enjoys and favors this state. Allah is the Creator of horizons beyond human conception and imagination. Often outer and material constrictions can be the key to opening insights and doors of inner knowledge, expansion and deeper contentment.

Call upon Al-Bāsit at times of restriction and constriction, and visualize His limitless and infinite mercy and horizons. Contemplate the need for expansion and restriction and the balance of life's experiences between them.

AL-KHĀFID
The Debaser

From the root *khafada*: to lower, to humble, depress, debase. It does not appear as a name in the Qur'an, but is inferred from its verbal form.

Allah is the real cause behind the powers which bring about honor as well as dishonor. Al-Khāfid brings about debasement out of compassion for His mighty presence and greatness. The *nafs* always resists debasement and humility, but the *mu'min* will derive great spiritual benefit from this condition if he is sensitive and reads His mercy.

Whenever one experiences injustice, haughtiness and arrogance, Al-Khāfid will come into discernible effect.

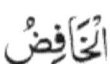

AL-RĀFI`
The Exalter

From the root *rafa`a*: to raise up, exalt, uplift and elevate. Al-Rāfi` appears in the Qur'an as He Who has the power to elevate (13:2; 55:7).

Allah is the most exalted Lord of all creation. He raises high the believer through hope and good expectation. Allah elevates pure hearts for their submission and high expectation of Him, through which they witness higher and subtler realms of greatness and lights.

Meditate and reflect upon how the root of honor lies in humility and subtlety, and how human arrogance and self-aggrandizement can bring about debasement, where the lower self belongs.

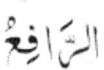

AL-MU'IZZ
The Honorer

From the same root as Al-`Aziz, `azza: to be rare, precious; to be powerful, potent, strong, mighty.

Allah bestows honor, dignity and power on those who are accepted into His proximity, and thus the glow of His great qualities. Whoever abases himself and maintains *taqwā* will be honored by Allah the holder of true glory. The more sincere our *islām*, *īmān* and *ihsān*, the more honored we are in the eyes of Allah and His creation.

Whenever the seeker experiences any honor or acknowledgement he must relate it back to the real Honorer, Al-Mu`izz, and admit His favor and grace.

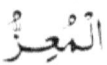

AL-MUDHILL
The Abaser

From the root *dhalla*: to be abject, humble, low, base, inglorious, despicable; and *adhalla*: to humiliate, abase; to break or subdue.

Allah has created Adam and his offspring to be submissive and dependant on His grace and favor. Thus the arrogant ones will be abased. Human beings experience imperfection because Allah in His Mercy will always give us cause to recognize our needs and insignificance. Thus we can truly glorify the All-Perfect and Mighty Lord Who covers human weaknesses, and propels us towards His perfection.

When we recognize false honor assumed by human beings, the *mu'min* sees the hallmark of Al-Mudhill next to it. When the seeker accepts *Dhūll* (humility), Al-Mu`izz will cover him and vice versa.

AL-SAMĪ`
The All-Hearing

From the root *sami`a*: to Hear, to listen, to Hearken to.

Allah hears the sounds and silence of all His creation. He hears without ears, sees without eyes and knows without intellect. In the human being all these organs are small samples and reflections of His abilities. Allah hears and responds appropriately. Human hearing can only occur through disturbances and vibrations in space impinging upon the instrument of the ear. Allah hears the source, cause and meaning of all calls, and is the Destination of all that has been transmitted.

Al-Samī` is the All-Hearing and Responding. So call upon Him regularly, constantly and persistently, with courteous patience and high expectation. Al-Samī` is the All-Hearing, Who knows what the truth is behind your supplication, even if you do not yet know.

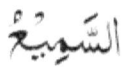

AL-BASĪR
The All-Seeing

From the root *basara*: to look at, see, perceive; *basīrah*, the faculty of insight, cognition.

Allah is the source of all sight and cognition, visible and invisible. Al-Basīr witnesses what is evident and what is hidden. Human sight is a modest reflection and sample of Al-Basīr, needing both light and the instrument to perceive light and shadow, the eyes.

To enhance sight, meaning, and understanding, we call upon Al-Basīr. He alone grants insights.

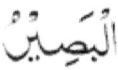

AL-HAKAM
The Judge

From the root *hakama*: to exercise authority; to govern; to judge; *hikmah* is also wisdom. Allah is also described as Khayr al-Hākimīn (7:87) and Ahkam al-Hākimīn, 'The Wisest of Judges' (11:45.)

Allah is the source of justice, wisdom and perfect judgment. Al-Hakam confirms His Will with authority and will judge His creation according to their actions and intentions through His decrees; thus all creation will experience its just destiny.

Reliable justice can be understood by human beings when the self has been tethered by the virtues of modesty, courage and wisdom.

AL-`ADL
The All-Just

From `adala`: to act justly; to treat equitably. Al-`Adl is not found in the Qur'an but inferred from ayats like 6:115.

The essence of justice and equity is a quality of the Creator, Allah, the Exalted. To understand the perfection of divine justice we need to understand *tawhīd* at all levels, i.e. the active and causal *tawhīd* and intricate balance and connection between all attributes and names and the unique all-permeating essence. To live and acknowledge His absolute justice is to acknowledge the truth of our total submission, reliance and trust in Him.

The ultimate justice is the sincere confession that creation is totally dependent upon the Creator and as such is all His. This is true justice. Every situation is subject to and measured by His justice, which often differs from human expectations or judgment. What may appear as delayed justice is Allah cloaking His justice in clemency and patience.

AL-LATĪF
The Subtle

From *latafa*: to be kindly, to be fine, elegant, graceful; *latīf* is gracious, kind, the opposite of gross or dense, and it also means acutely insightful; *lutf* is subtlety, gentleness.

Allah is the subtle power and light behind every manifestation, seen, heard, smelt, tasted or touched, known and unknown. His subtlety (*lutf*) permeates all creation soft and hard, evident or concealed, sentient or otherwise.

The subtle grace of *lutf* flows throughout creation as a force of gatheredness and dispersion, for all apparent opposites in the universe are permeated by the unique energy of *lutf*, which is an aspect of His love. When engulfed by outer action and grossness, call upon Ya Latīf, for sublime upliftment. His *lutf* will uplift you from physicality to subtlety, from the outer to the inner, and you will see the inner meaning of your outer action.

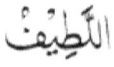

AL-KHABĪR
The All-Cognizant

From the root *khabara*: to experience; to know thoroughly; to possess expertise; *khabar*, pl. *akhbār*, is news, tidings.

Allah is aware of whatever is in the heaven and the earth. His Knowledge encompasses all aspects of existence, inner and outer, subtle and gross. Nothing ever moves or happens in existence without His knowledge and according to His decrees. To call upon Al-Khabīr is to gain clarity from confusion by deep cognition and understanding.

The need for appropriate insight, expertise and relevant skill to deal with any situation is fulfilled by Al-Khabīr. Microscopic, telescopic and subtler insights are small springs filled by the river of light called Al-Khabīr.

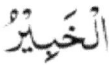

AL-HALĪM
The Clement

From *halama*, to dream, and *haluma*, to be gentle, forbearing. *Hilm* is clemency, forbearance, gentleness.

Allah is the most tolerant regarding the shortcomings and wrongdoings of His creation. He allows His creation new opportunities for correcting their conduct – for His desire is *taqwā* and knowledge of Him, not punishment. It is He Who knows the disobedience and misconduct of His creation yet, even so, He does not respond with anger and swift punishment. He is the Most Forbearing, Forgiving and Patient.

To remember Al-Halīm is to enhance the quality of clemency within us, whilst realizing His immense generosity and patience.

AL-`ADHĪM
The Magnificent

From the root `aDhūma`: to be great, mighty, vast, powerful. Dhū Fadlin `Adhīm, Possessor of Sublime Grace (3:172), is a Divine Name from the same root.

Allah's greatness is beyond boundaries, measures or descriptions. We consider the prophets to be great in their human character, qualities and capacities, because we have had a glimpse of their attributes drawn from Al-Adhīm. Allah's Magnificence is such that His command will always apply, and any resistance is of no consequence. His Magnificence encompasses all the known and unknown, manifest and unmanifest realities. His Greatness transcends the limitations of our minds, and thus helps us ascend to higher realms of light.

AL-GHAFŪR
The All-Forgiving

Like Al-Ghaffār, this Name derives from *ghafara,* meaning to cover; to pardon; to veil; to conceal. *Al-Ghafūr* covers repeated errors, while *Al-Ghaffār* covers and forgives all different types of errors. Allah forgives multitudes of wrongdoing in a recurring fashion. Ghāfir Al-Dhanb, The Forgiver of Wrong-doing (40:3), is also a Divine Name from the same root.

Allah conceals and covers the faults of the *mu'mins* for He knows how best to bring His sincere subjects to Him. To forgive is to renew opportunities and give new space and energy for further spiritual awakening.

Whenever one has continually made the same errors, call upon Him Who has witnessed them and abandon that habit. Al-Ghafūr forgives multiple recurring errors.

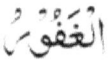

AL-SHAKŪR
The Grateful

From the root *shakara*: to give thanks, to be grateful, content, pleased; *shukr* is gratitude. Al-Shakūr manifests through the multiplication of rewards. Al-Shākir, the Grateful One, is from the same root (2:158).

Allah rewards and acknowledges appropriate deeds by means of which the seeker is drawn closer. He acknowledges the deeds of the believer by rewarding him many times more than the action itself, with a continuous flow of gratitude leading to trust and contentment.

The inner state of gratitude in us brings about a positive good feeling that is conducive to the increase in higher quality surrender and faith. To express gratitude to the One brings about contentment which leads to the door of illumination.

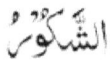

AL-`ALĪ
The Most High

From the root `alī: to rise high; to be elevated, lofty; to mount up. *Al-A`la* – The Most High, is from the same root (87:1).

Allah transcends all measures of low and high. He is the Creator of all the heavenly spheres; He is beyond them, yet controls and rules them. Al-`Alī is a station that is above all perceivable and conceivable states by the human mind. The ultimate mercy is that while He is the most sublime and high, He is also closer to you than the jugular vein. His elevation is not due to distance but to absolute purity and subtlety.

Only the wholesome heart can reflect Al-`Alī. When a divine opening, insight or knowledge comes to you, confirm its source, Al-`Alī, for it has descended upon you from the Most High.

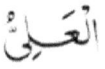

AL-KABĪR
The Incomprehensibly Great

From the root *kabura*, to be great; to grow, increase; to be big or vast. *Akbar* is greater or most great.

Allah is larger than largeness and vaster than vastness, thus transcending the mind and our ability to visualize His true station. Allah's glory, beauty, power and majesty are all beyond greatness. Al-Kabīr relates to Allah's sanctity before creation and after it. *Kabīr* also implies perfection and the ultimate and maximum limit in desirable attributes.

Calling upon Al-Kabīr is an admission of our limitation, submission and a call for awakening to His greatness. Whatever we have considered to be great or of significance in our world is inconsequential; therefore, at all times, *'Allahu Akbar'* is the voice of intelligence.

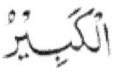

AL-HAFĪDH
The Preserver

From the root *hafidha*: to keep; to guard; to preserve; to protect; to take care of and watch over.

Allah's primal patterns and 'Tablet' are ever preserved. His original ways and decrees protect His creation in the most appropriate manner on their journey. It is Al-Hafidh who Helps and safeguards His creation during their existence. All creation is accountable for actions and interactions, and people will experience aspects of their deeds. Al-Hafidh keeps us in *taqwā*, in spite of our lower tendencies.

Whenever we feel vulnerable and weak, Al-Hafidh is there to cover our frailty and faults.

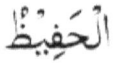

AL-MUQĪT
The Sustainer

From the root *qāta*: to nourish, feed; to sustain; it also relates to awareness and ability.

Allah has created what is appropriate to nourish, maintain and develop His creation. Allah sustains all creations through their attraction, absorption, retention, consumption, maturation and procreation. The Sustainer reflects the Everlasting, which all creation celebrates and desires.

We call upon Al-Muqīt in all matters of sustenance and ongoingness.

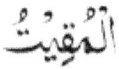

AL-HASĪB
The Reckoner

From the root *hasaba*: to reckon; to consider; to count; to believe; to suppose. Sarī' al-Hisāb, the Swift in Reckoning, is another version of this Attribute (40:17). Hasīb also implies sufficiency.

Allah is the master treasurer of all quantities and qualities. Their measure and their whereabouts throughout creation are known and kept by Him. Al-Hasīb is He Who Suffices His Creation. All reckoning and measure emanate from Him. When the believer relies sincerely and entirely upon Allah, then all other considerations will be insignificant. Distraction and false security will vanish and the light of excellence will wipe away all sadness.

When one is truly reliant upon Al-Hasīb, with certainty and sincerity, then the call '*Hasbi Allah*' (Allah is enough for me) will yield its promised response.

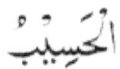

AL-JALĪL
The Majestic

From the root *jalla*: to be glorious, evident, effulgent, shining, majestic, lofty; sublime. *Jallala* means to honor or exalt. Al-Jalīl does not appear in the Qur'an in this form but as *Dhū al-Jalāli wa al-Ikrām*: The Possessor of Glory and Nobility.

Allah is the Source of sublime majesty and glory. Al-Jalīl encompasses all these lofty attributes to the zone of transcendence and pure essence. These are unique beams of light emanating from the original Divine One, Who is worthy of glory and majesty beyond human reckoning. His majesty is balanced by His beauty and thereby relates to His perfection.

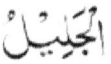

AL-KARĪM
The Most Generous

From the root *karuma*: to be noble, superior in generosity; to be highly esteemed, valued; to be excellent, generous, and magnanimous. The name Al-Akram, The Most Generous, from the same root, is also in the Qur'an. From the same root comes *karm*, that is, grapevines, generous in production.

Al-Karīm is He Who gives more than what is asked. Allah is the Source of all movement and light upon which all life depends, and thus He is the Source of all giving, the Most Generous, the perfect master.

Whenever one has a need or desire one can only call upon the ever-present, generous Al-Karīm.

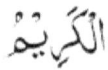

AL-RAQĪB
The All-Vigilant

From the root *raqaba*: to observe, notice; to watch, guard. Al-Raqīb watches over His creation knowingly, protectively and effectively.

    Allah is ever-watchful over all His Kingdoms. No intention or action is ever missed by His Omnipresence. Al-Raqīb is the essence and center of awareness, which witnesses and thus responds according to individual conditions, needs and abilities.

    Whenever there is a need for watchfulness and care, one calls upon Him and enters into watchfulness (*murāqabah*). In this state the seeker transcends thought and awareness and enters His proximity.

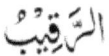

AL-MUJĪB
The Responder

From *ajāba*: to answer, reply; to comply, fulfill; which in turn derives from *jāba*: to pierce, penetrate; cut; to travel, explore. *Jawāb* is a reply or answer.

Allah is the answerer to all who call on Him, most generously, according to real needs. He is the Mujīb al-Da`wāt, the Answerer of all supplications. The compassionate Lord has created out of love and therefore responds to sincere submission. Al-Mujīb responds to the call from all, at all times, according to His perfect discernment.

With Allah, the call and its answer are instantaneous. In order for us to get close to that understanding we need to be in constant awareness and courtesy to Al-Mujīb.

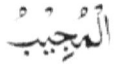

AL-WĀSI`
The All-Encompassing

From the root *wasi`a*: to be wide, ample, vast; to contain; to encompass; to comprehend.

Allah's dominion is limitless and His capacity for knowledge, mercy and generosity is boundless. Our needs and visions are limited by our existential perceptions. He encompasses all that we need, know and perceive. His wealth is beyond limit, that is, vast (*wāsi*).

Whenever one experiences the vastness of space and other similar attributes, one is close to Al-Wāsi`, and can call upon the Creator of all vastness.

AL-HAKĪM
The Most Wise

From *hakama*: to exercise authority; to rule; to judge between. The noun *hikmah* means wisdom, correct judgment, and discernment. The Prophet (*pbuh*) said: 'The root of *hikmah* is *taqwā* of Allah.'

At all times Allah's wisdom and the power to implement it encompasses everything. Al-Hakīm's perfect knowledge enables Him to decree the perfect ways for perfectly appropriate outcomes. His justice and compassion are 'companions' to His wisdom.

Whenever one is in need of wisdom and appropriate knowledge, one knocks upon the doors of Al-Hakīm, sincerely and humbly.

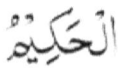

AL-WADŪD
The All-Loving

From *wadda*: to love, like; to wish; to be fond of; *mawaddah* is affection or friendship.

Allah's love penetrates the entire creation and is felt most by His submissive lovers and worshippers. Al-Wadūd is most intimate, close and gentle to all and wishes the best for all creations. This divine affection and love is the cause of much bonding and relationships in creation.

When one is in need of solace or is experiencing His subtle affection, one reinforces the power of the presence of Al-Wadūd by calling this Name.

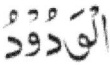

AL-MAJĪD
The Most Glorious

From *majada:* to be glorious, exalted; to excel in glory. *Majīd* means glorious, splendid, illustrious, noble in essence, dignified, and vast in generosity.

Allah is the master of all glory and the source of every manifestation of honor and mercy. Al-Majīd relates to Allah, whose essence is most noble, whose actions are most beautiful, and whose generosity is vast beyond measure.

Whenever a situation reminds you of glory, call upon and celebrate the Most Glorious.

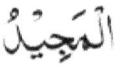

AL-BĀ'ITH
The Resurrector

From *ba'atha*: to send, dispatch; to arouse, awaken; to raise, resurrect.

Allah is the source of life on this earth and will resurrect creation after they have experienced death. It is Al-Bā'ith Who sends forth His creation from their graves, in order for them to experience what they have earned in the Hereafter. The Prophet (*pbuh*) said, 'You will be resurrected in the state that you left this world.' Perfect justice prevails in His kingdom.

To remember Al-Bā'ith is to pronounce one's faith, because we are accountable for our intentions and actions, and will therefore be resurrected after this life, and reap the rewards of His generosity.

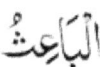

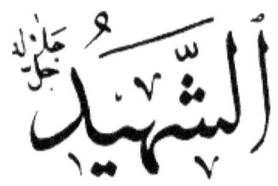

AL-SHAHĪD
The All-Witnessing

From the root *shahida*: to be present at; to bear witness or testimony; to confirm; to acknowledge. *Shahādah*, the testimony of faith, as evinced by the *kalima: Lā ilāha illā Allāh Muhammadun Rasūl Allāh* – the ultimate truth of *tawhīd*.

Allah is present at all times, seeing, hearing and knowing. When Allah's witnessing relates to the visible world, Allah will manifest to us more as Al-'Alīm, and when it is to do with the unseen, we call upon Allah, Al-Khabīr. In all cases Allah is Al-Shahīd. He is aware of all actions and intentions. The *Dīn* and all prophetic practices and disciplines enhance the quality of our awareness and the witnessing of Him – the All-Aware.

For the unawakened person the witnesser within is dormant or very limited; so call upon Him whose *Shahādah* is all-encompassing.

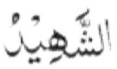

AL-HAQQ
The Absolute Truth

From the root *haqqa*: to be true, right, just, valid. *Haqīqah* is truth, reality. *Al-haqqah* is the Day of Judgment when truth will be known.

From One absolute Truth emanates infinite varieties of realities, manifestations and experiences. Truth is one and other realities vary constantly and are short-lived. Al-Haqq enables us to distinguish right from wrong, good from bad, truth from falsehood, the real, everlasting and self-sustaining from the fleeting. Haqq is the reference point within us which will shed light upon relative experiences.

The highest truth is a Divine Attribute; thus Al-Haqq is called upon to reveal falsehood and that which will change. He, Allah, does not.

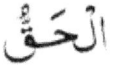

AL-WAKĪL
The Guardian Trustee

From *wakala*: to entrust, to commit anything to another's keeping; to delegate (e.g. a power of attorney). *Tawakkul* is trusting and entrusting your affairs to Allah.

Allah disposes of our affairs most efficiently and dependably according to His perfect decrees. When Al-Wakīl is empowered over all our affairs then the journey will certainly lead to the Source and original light. Allah is the truly trustworthy, and thus the perfect One to delegate one's affairs to. He is the perfect guardian Who knows what is appropriate for creation to reach the optimum state of knowledge and realization.

When we are gifted with the need and the support of Allah, we call upon Al-Wakīl and then rest confident of the outcome.

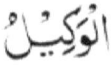

AL-QAWĪ
The Most Strong

From the root *qawiya*: to excel in strength; to be tough. *Quwwah* is power, potency, and force. Dhū al-Quwwah, The Possessor of Power, is another Name from the same root.

Allah's power and strength is beyond measure, and His capacity to exercise that power appears in the subtle, spiritual, as well as in the physical domains. All powers are aspects and manifestations of Allah's *Quwwah*. Thus, contemplating all the different physical, chemical, biological, electro-magnetic, subtle/spiritual and all other powers could lead us to the door of the One, All-Powerful, Al-Qawī.

Weak as creation is, we need to call upon the fountainhead of all power and strength: Al-Qawī – Allah.

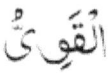

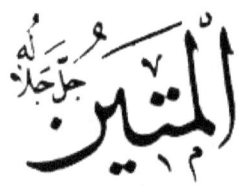

AL-MATĪN
The Firm

From the root *matana*: to be firm, solid, strong.

The source of absolute firmness and the power to withstand is Al-Matīn. He is ever-reliable in His strength, power and capacity and is not given to any weakness, inadequacy or faults. His firmness can be materially manifest as well as most subtle and unseen.

Whenever one is in need of steadfastness and resolve one calls upon the ever-present Attribute of Al-Matīn.

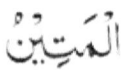

AL-WALĪ
The Patron

From the root *waliya*: to be near; to befriend; to be a patron of someone; to manage; to govern. In Islam a sage, saint or gnostic is often referred to as a *walī* (pl. *awliya'*), implying that they have befriended Allah through submission and worship and He has accepted them close to Him.

Allah is an ever-reliable and available helper for seekers of truth. Al-Walī is the closest and ultimately most trusted and loyal friend to the believer. It is through this Attribute that mercy, victory and guidance emanate. For the true Muslim in the religion of Islam, the most worthy *walī* is the Prophet (*pbuh*) himself.

Whoever seeks an ever-reliable friendship and source of comfort, call upon the ultimate *Walī*.

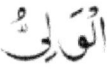

AL-HAMĪD
The Praiseworthy

From *hamida*: to praise, eulogize, commend, exalt. Allah has the highest desirable qualities and thus He is the true worthy recipient of all true praise. Several names derive from this root: *Mahmūd*, praised; *Hamīd*, worthy of praise; *Ahmad*, most praiseworthy; *Muhammad*, highly lauded.

Allah is the ultimate praiseworthy and all praise ascends to Him as has been made known to us by Him. Whatever is praiseworthy, its Creator is even more worthy of praise. It is also He Who has given us the primal knowledge of what to praise and desire. Allah praises himself and manifests himself to us through beauty, majesty and other glorious attributes.

Whatever you praise you are ultimately praising Allah, and when you are in a state of praise you are calling to Al-Hamīd.

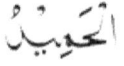

AL-MUHSĪ
The Appraiser

From the root *ahsā*: to calculate; take account of; to know numbers, varieties, qualities and inventories. Al-Muhsī is used in the Qur'an, in its verbal form (58:6).

Allah knows everything to do with His creations, their types, species, qualities, quantities, potentials, abilities, limitations, etc. Al-Muhsī is the record-keeper and ultimate expert in the knowledge of what goes on in Creation. Allah knows the number of heartbeats and all what goes on, seen and hidden. The 'Tablet' represents His databank and future designs.

Al-Muhsī maintains knowledge and control of everything in His kingdom.

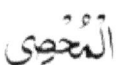

AL-MUBDI'
The Originator

From *bada'a*: to begin, start; to bring forth; to initiate, originate. Al-Mubdi' appears in the Qur'an in its verbal form (85:13).

Allah brought forth creation from non-existence and will cause it to return to Him. Allah's creations have beginnings, ends and purpose, and are sustained and empowered by His eternal presence and powers. He is the most efficient and perfect creator of all things known and unknown. Their origin and end is designed by Him.

Calling upon the Perfect Originator is the courteous start to human endeavors in this World.

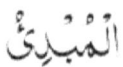

AL-MU`ĪD
The Returner

From `ada: to return; to restore; to bring back; to repeat. Al-Mu`īd appears in the Qur'an in its verbal form (85:13).

Allah's universe is caught within movement: emanating and returning, and constantly fluctuating between opposites. The Returner will bring creation back to life after death, onto a new phase. In that state all beings will re-live what they have earned in this life. Allah is the constant factor behind all life and change and thus only He has the power of returning everything back to its origin or to a new cycle of growth or decline.

The return in the Hereafter is based on the state of departure from this world. Those who have awakened to His Light in this world will live by His Light in the next. As for those engulfed in the darkness of the beasts within, they will also experience those beasts once again.

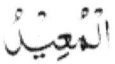

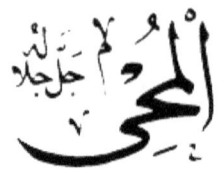

AL-MUHYĪ
The Life-Giver

From the root *hayya*: to live. *Ahyā* is to give life; to preserve, restore, or save lives. *Muhyī al-Dīn* (a given name) is he who brings the religion (*Dīn*) back to life. *Yahya* (John) is another given name which comes from this same root. Al-Muhyī appears in the Qur'an in its verbal form (30:50).

Allah is the originator of life's experience, the source of all creational manifestations. Al-Muhyī is the energy source of the light behind life. The mystery of life is gifted to creation and is based on constant change supported and sustained by the ever-constant provider. Al-Muhyī has brought this earth to life after it was inert. He also brings eternal life to the heart through knowledge and enlightenment once the self has been subdued.

Call upon the Al-Muhyī to increase awareness of the mystery and meaning of real life.

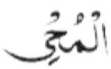

AL-MUMĪT
The Death-Giver

From *māta*: to die, perish; to subside. Al-Mumīt appears in the Qur'an in its verbal form (2:28).

Allah is the Creator of the experience of death, from which no living being is ever deprived or excluded. It is the power of Al-Mumīt that will terminate the experience of earthly life through an angelic agency. No living creature will escape death at the appointed time and place. Sleep is nothing other than a short experience resembling death. The remembrance of death energizes the believer to pierce the veils of ignorance, and frightens the disbelievers.

Glorify Al-Mumīt and you will come closer to the light of Al-Muhyī (the Life Giver); these two Attributes reflect each other.

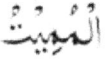

AL-HAYY
The Ever-Living

From the same root as Al-Muhyī, *hayya*: to live. All life on earth is a short form of the next phase of timelessness.

Allah, from Whom all life emanates, is Ever-Living. He is the bestower of life as experienced in time. He is not subject to time, decay or death. Al-Hayy is beyond all matters of change in existence. He is the enduring eternal light illuminating all lights.

Our short life in this world is a window onto Al-Hayy. Call upon Him to put in perspective our false expectations of this life.

AL-QAYYŪM
The All-Sustaining

From the root *qāma*: to stand fast, or firm (not requiring external support). From the same root we have: *qawm*, nation; *iqāmah*, the call to stand for prayer; *maqām*: rank or station, as well as mausoleum.

Allah is the Source of all subsistence and existence. He bestows all stations and states. Al-Qayyūm is self-supporting and self-sustaining, firm in His Will, and rules over and cares for His dominion and creation by Himself. He has no need nor desires whilst creation always has needs and desires. Thus, we need to call upon Him.

Often supplication of Al-Qayyūm is combined with Al-Hayy (the Ever-Living) as in, *ya Hayy ya Qayyūm*.

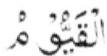

AL-WĀJID
The Manifestor

From *wājada*: to find; to uncover; to meet, encounter; to invent; to experience or feel.

Nothing is ever concealed from Allah for He has brought forth everything in this universe by His own power and command. From non-existence Allah has brought forth all imaginable combinations of creation and experience, subtle and gross. Al-Wājid is the founder of everything in existence, and has the power over all that exists, both manifest and otherwise. For Him everything is evident and clear.

Calling Al-Wājid is to call upon the bringer forth from non-existence.

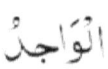

AL-MĀJID
The Most Splendid

From the same root as Al-Mājid, *mājada*: to excel in glory, honor, elevation and precious attributes.

Allah is the source of all splendor and magnificence, the most excellent and glorious. All the beautiful attributes and actions belong to Al-Mājid. His qualities are most desirable, lofty and longed for. Al-Mājid is the most sublime, pure and high in position of excellence.

Any glorious manifestation or experience is a worthy reminder of Al-Mājid. All creation aspires to this lofty state.

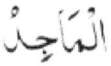

AL-WĀHID
The One

From *wahada*: to be one, alone; to be unmatched, incomparable, unequalled.

It is in Allah, Al-Wāhid, that all the diverse Divine Attributes meet. The singular root of all multiplicity and diversity. Al-Wāhid is unique, all-encompassing and indivisible, the origin of all attributes relating to actions, qualities and other names, in short, the One. The *mu'min* reflects in his heart's mirror this Name in that he acts, judges, sees, hears, etc., yet he still refers to himself as 'I', the same 'one'.

All plurality in this world meets in Al-Wāhid, Who will bring the invoker to the One Light behind all Names.

AL-AHAD
The Absolute One

From the same root as Al-Wāhid, Al-Ahad means: the only One, unique, incomparable, singular.

Allah is not subject to numbers or plurality. He is other than that which can be identified or defined, the One independent reality upon Whom all others depend and draw. Al-Ahad is of pure essence without manifesting any attributes. There is no comparison or similarity to this sublime Truth: *Ahadiyyah*.

Calling upon Al-Ahad is calling upon the Absolute One, beyond all description. The invocation usually combines Al-Wāhid (The One) with Al-Ahad.

AL-SAMAD
The Self-Sufficient

From *samada*: to have recourse to; to withstand; to be sublime; to be steadfast; to be everlasting; to be self-supporting.

Allah is everlasting, self-sustaining, self-contained and most sublime. Al-Samad is the authority to which requirements are referred, for He is the source of reliance. All needs and calls are addressed to Al-Samad. He is the master and the One, Who is forever sought after, for He endures beyond time. All creation needs Al-Samad, yet He is in no need.

The call of Al-Samad will bring back the truth in dependency on Him. Often supplication is made combining Al-Fard (the Unique One) with Al-Samad, as in *ya Fard, ya Samad*.

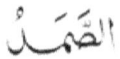

AL-QĀDIR
The Most Able

From *qadara*: to be able (to do something); to prevail; to determine. *Qudrah* is power, ability. Al-Qādir – The Able, Prevailing One – from the same root, is also a Divine Name. *Laylat al-Qadr* is the Night of Determination or Power.

Allah is the source of all power, possibility and ability. Al-Qādir has the power over all created entities regarding all matters, known and unknown. His power is perfect, efficient and appropriate for each situation and His abilities are indefinable by creation. He achieves effortlessly and according to His Will.

When powerless and unable to face the task ahead, call at the door of Al-Qādir.

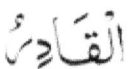

AL-MUQTADIR
The All-Powerful

The root meaning is the same as Al-Qādir: powerful, prevailing.

Al-Muqtadir is the superlative of Al-Qādir. Al-Muqtadir makes manifest His power and ability and He acts and brings forth according to His knowledge and wisdom, over and above secondary abilities. There are many levels of powers and abilities, both qualitative and quantitative.

Al-Muqtadir is the Supremely Able. He represents the ultimate in capabilities and abilities.

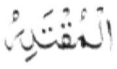

AL-MUQADDIM
The Expediter

From *qaddama*: to bring forth; to precede; to present; to advance. Al-Muqaddim appears in its verbal form (50:28).

Allah possesses the power over time and can expedite matters earlier than expected or imagined. Al-Muqaddim had brought forth the creation of heaven and earth and then embellished them with the Adamic creation. He makes manifest and presents to creation what they have within themselves as potential and possible.

Call upon Al-Muqaddim when you want to expedite or speed up a goodly deed.

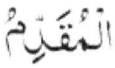

AL-MU'AKHKHIR
The Postponer

From *akhkhara*: to delay, defer; to remain behind. The *Ākhirah* is the Hereafter or Next Life. Al-Mu'akhkhir appears in the Qur'an in the verbal form (11:8).

The Creator of time has total mastery over it. Existential events and occurrences can be delayed as He Wills. Al-Mu'akhkhir's postponement of justice gives a chance to creation to remedy wrongdoing, otherwise we would perish. The postponer gives us opportunities for repentance and the return to His path, so that we experience His perfect mercy and justice.

Whenever a believer supplicates to Allah and experiences delay in His answer, he knows that the results will come later, in an even better way than he had hoped, for Allah times all things perfectly.

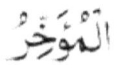

AL-AWWAL
The First

From *ala*: to return; to be before; *awwal* is the first, the beginning; *ala* means the foremost.

Allah was first before anything and was eternal in essence before any other existences. He is the same now, even after creation. He is constantly the First and all existences perish except Him. He neither ages nor changes; He was and is before everything, within everything, and after everything.

By calling upon Al-Awwal one becomes properly sensitive and aware at the start of events or situations.

AL-ĀKHIR
The Last

From the same root as Al-Mu'akhkhir: *ākhir* is the last, beyond the end; hence *ākhirah* is the Hereafter.

Allah maintains creation and His light will continue after creation ends, thus He is the Last. Allah's Attribute of The Last is without end since He has no creational beginning nor end. He is the First, the Last, the Manifest and Non-Manifest, for He is beyond all matters of time and space. The whole cosmos rests in His palm.

Contemplate Al-Ākhir, who is forever lasting, when we experience departure and change.

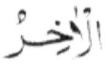

AL-DHĀHIR
The Manifest

From the root *dhāhara*: to be or become manifest apparent, clear, evident. *Dhūhr* means noon and also the midday prayer.

Allah's power of Will and Command makes manifest all existence. The divine light interacting within existence results in manifestations and experiences. The entire cosmos appeared due to that Essential Light which remains with it and guides it to its destiny. All cosmic manifestations have within them meanings and the divine essence.

Whenever you see something that reminds you of Allah, you are actually witnessing Al-Dhāhir, veiling the Al-Bātin (The Concealed).

AL-BĀTIN
The Concealed

From *batana*: to be concealed inside; to be hidden (within the inner lining). *Batn* means belly, while *batin* is the innermost.

It is Allah whose subtle and unseen powers are behind all outer realities. Allah is the hidden root of everything. From the One essence manifest multitudes of attributes and finally experienced realities. Physical and other realities are activated by the subtle force of the inner, hidden power of the One. The illumined being sees the subtle as well as the manifest together, for the truth is only One.

When one experiences or witnesses the subtle meaning behind the form or event, a facet of Al-Bātin is being revealed. When you seek the meaning behind certain situations call upon Al-Bātin.

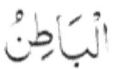

AL-WĀLĪ
The Governor

From *waliya*: to be near; to guard; to befriend; to govern, have command over; and *wāliya*: to be a friend, patron; to Help. Al-Wālī does not appear in the Qur'an as such, but *Wālī* frequently appears as a divine title (42:9).

Al-Wālī is the center that manages all creational affairs and implements Allah's decrees. All created beings experience their appropriate destinies justly and perfectly. When an enlightened being is referred to as a *wālī*, it means a close friend of Allah and true reflector of the truth: a saint. This being has subjected his will to that of Allah, and thus there is no friction or discontentment – a perfect friendship.

When seeking the ultimate guardian friend, call *Ya Wālī*.

AL-MUTA`ĀLĪ
The Most Exalted

From the root *'Alā* : to be high, lofty, exalted; to be proud. Al-Muta`ālī appears in the Qur'an in the form of Al-Muta`al (13:9).

Allah is higher than any measurable height and is exalted beyond all limits of exaltation. Al-Muta`ālī is of utmost glory and is exalted in all His attributes beyond comprehension. It is He Who knows the seen and the unseen, the past, present and future. He is beyond reach and yet the closest. To understand Him we need to transcend the mind and its limitations.

Call upon Al-Muta`ālī and witness limitless exaltation.

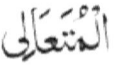

AL-BARR
The Benefactor

From the root *barra*: to be reverent, pious; to be dutiful, devoted, charitable; to be obedient; to treat well; to be truthful. *Barr* is correct, kind, proper, well; while *birr* is reverence, godliness.

Allah is the source of constant goodness and tolerance. His goodness is evident for those in cautious awareness and who see Him as the *Rabb* (Lord) of all. Allah's generosity to the virtuous is by increasing their light and knowledge, and thus their inner contentment. As for the wrongdoers, He forgives them and shows them mercy.

Al-Barr is the ever-available source of reliable and loving response.

AL-TAWWĀB
The Most Accepting of Repentance

From *taba*: to turn (to Allah) in repentance, to regret at heart, and return with no excuse. Allah is *Qabil al-Tawbah*: The Acceptor Of Repentance (9:104).

He is the ever-present Who accepts whomever returns to Him with regret and repentance. Repentance can be due to fear of punishment, or in anticipation of rewards, or simply because Allah is the One worthy of it. Allah always rewards those who have returned to Him with His mercy and grace. Al-Tawwāb forever covers human errors and frailties with His power, generosity and life.

To call upon Al-Tawwāb is to realize His infinite generosity, compassion and forgiveness. It is the door to renewal.

AL-MUNTAQIM
The Avenger

From the root *naqama*: to loathe, disapprove. *Intaqama* is to reject; to avenge or take revenge. Al-Muntaqim appears in the Qur'an as a derivative, that is Dhū al-Intiqam, the Possessor of Retribution.

Allah balances wrong action by bringing about its equivalent consequence. No act goes unnoticed or remains without its result. The arrogant and wrongdoer bring upon themselves the deserved revenge and disasters in both this world and the next. Allah's generosity is such that He allows periods of respite for reflection and repentance in order to return to truth and the path of submission, modesty, wisdom, and justice. If this natural course is not followed then the result is simply misfortune.

This Attribute relate to the experience of adversity, trial and human affliction. These emanate from Al-Muntaqim as a balancer to bring us back to equilibrium. This attribute is complementary to the quality of *na`ma'*, which means amenity, comfort and ease.

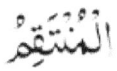

AL-`AFŪW
The Pardoner

From `afa: to erase or wipe out the trace of something; to pardon, forgive. *Al-`Afūw* is He Who pardons and erases past wrongs.

Allah covers our weakness by His mercy and obliterates the traces of our past wrong actions. He renews, purifies and gives new opportunities. Allah eradicates the consequence of evil acts and overlooks wrong action of those who return in submission, cautious awareness, and sincere supplication.

Truly He is Al-`Afūw and the Source of renewed hope and illumined fresh opportunities.

AL-RA'ŪF
The Most Affectionate

From *ra'afa*: to be compassionate, merciful; to exercise affection and gentleness.

Allah is constant in His gentleness and compassion. His original love and mercy encompass all of creation, believers and non-believers alike. It is His *ra'fah* that is reflected in a mother's unconditional love and gentleness for her offspring. All aspects of compassion and gentleness emanate from this Divine Attribute without which life would not continue. The rewards of Al-Muntaqim (The Avenger) and Al-Muhsī (The Appraiser) is in experiencing the presence and light of Al-Ra'ūf in all circumstances.

Al-Ra'ūf is the most patient and understanding One, so call upon Him when these qualities are needed.

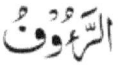

MĀLIK AL-MULK
The Master of The Kingdom

Both *malik* and *mulk* emanate from the same root: *malaka*, to possess power; to own a dominion; to prevail; to control, to be master of.

All worldly possessions and kingdoms are short-lived and change hands. The real and absolute King Who sustains, contains, and possesses all dominions is Allah. To Him belong the highest subtle realms as well as all physical and material creation. In Allah's hand lie expansion and constriction for He is the Lord Who can affect what He likes, the true master and king.

Whenever the notion of ownership or control arises, remember that Allah is in truth the ultimate and everlasting owner and inheritor. At best we are custodians, who have been given a short term loan.

DHŪ AL-JALĀLI WA AL-IKRĀM
The Master of Majesty and Nobility

From *jalla*, to be glorious, sublime, majestic. *Ikrām* is from *karuma*, meaning to honor; to be noble, generous, gracious, courteous, magnanimous.

Allah is the source of all glory, majesty, nobility and honor. His Majesty's commands are powerfully implemented and delivered. Allah's grace covers every domain from the beginning of time to its end.

Every majesty or honor emanates from the One Who truly exudes *Jalāl* and *Ikrām*. Each Attribute enhances and magnifies the other, for He is the Most Exalted.

AL-MUQSIT
The All-Equitable

From the root *aqsata*: to act justly or equitably. *Qist* is an equitable portion. Al-Muqsit appears in the Qur'an as a derivative (33:5).

Allah is the original source and cause of justice, balance, harmony, and all desirable outcomes and results. All creation is recompensed according to the extent of their acceptance and their fulfillment of the role for which they were created. The All-Equitable will give the tyrant as well as those in cautious awareness what they deserve. Allah is the most perfect judge and applier of His justice. We need to observe His ways through insights and pure vision, not according to our limited perception and changing values.

Everything in life is based on a measure and every action begets its appropriate outcome. To understand this call upon Al-Muqsit and witness His effective and perfect presence.

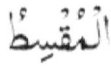

AL-JĀMI'
The Gatherer

From *jama`a*: to gather, collect, assemble; to compose; to unite.

The unifying power of the Creator has gathered to His Oneness all that which is in His kingdom. The heavens and the earth, the seen and unseen, the hard and the soft, the hot and cold, all opposites and all pluralities are in their appropriate places by the mystery of Al-Jāmi`. It is He Who maintains the absolute unity of the apparent infinite diversity in the universe. What appears as dispersion is already under the power of the *Jāmi*`.

Al-Jāmi` is the light which connects dispersion and diffusion.

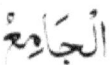

AL-GHANĪ
The Rich Beyond Need

From *ghaniya*: to be free from want; to have wealth; to be rich without needs.

Allah's wealth is boundless: He is the Source of all existential riches. Al-Ghanī is beyond any need. Allah's absolute wealth will not increase or reduce in any manner with His boundless generosity. Al-Ghanī is the absolutely self-sufficient, and thus beyond any description of wealth or treasure. He has created these as a means of reminding creation of their desires and to draw them to Him. He is the master of boundless cosmic treasures.

Whatever wealth one experiences or seeks, it emanates from the one and only true Source of wealth – Al-Ghanī.

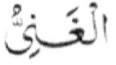

AL-MUGHNĪ
The Enricher

From the same root as Al-Ghanī. Al-Mughnī as such does not appear in the Qur'an but is a derivative (9:28). Allah, Who is the essence and root of all that is considered wealth, possesses the power to enrich whomever He wills.

Allah allows riches and desirable wealth to flow down to creation. His gifts are based on His ever-present mercy and generosity. The more a being is aware of the closeness of Allah and His treasury, the less desirous he or she becomes of material wealth and possessions. The ultimate wealth of the seeker is the knowledge that what he or she is seeking has already sought him or her, and is guiding him or her. Reliance on Allah is the ultimate wealth. In His hands are the keys to all known and unknown treasures.

All creation is impoverished and in need of calling upon Al-Mughnī. We all need sustenance, knowledge, guidance, contentment and happiness.

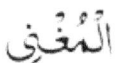

AL-MĀNI`
The Preventer

From *mana`a*: to prohibit, forbid, prevent; to deprive or withhold; to hinder. Al-Māni` does not appear in the Qur'an as such. To sustain life, the protective qualities of Al-Māni` are essential.

Allah prevents the disintegration and collapse of the universe. He protects His created systems at many levels by His cosmic powers. Yet no system goes on forever. It is the Al-Māni` that shields the believer from falling off the path of religion. He sets the boundaries and maintains the course for His creation.

The protection of Al-Māni` is called upon whenever one feels vulnerable and in need of defense, help, and containment.

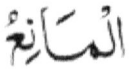

AL-DĀRR
The Bestower of Affliction

From *darra*: to afflict; to cause adversity and tribulation. This name does not appear in the Qur'an but is implied. Allah allows this Attribute to manifest, whilst He has already programmed in His living creation the desire to avoid it.

Life on this earth will be out of balance if every experience were good and desirable. Allah allows harm and affliction to come upon those who have committed wrong action as a reminder of transgression. The affliction is brought about by deviation from the path of virtue and the religion of Islam; and Allah in His mercy has given us the power and desire to avoid such outcomes. Thus punishment and affliction are motivating factors to return to the right path, both for individuals as well as societies. No one is spared this challenge, even if one tries to remain a bystander. The harm that is brought about by a few people can afflict many more.

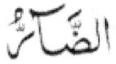

AL-NĀFI'
The Beneficial

From *nafa`a*: to be useful; to avail oneself, to be beneficial; to profit. Al-Nāfi' does not appear in the Qur'an except as a noun. We seek this Attribute at all times.

Allah is the source of all that is desired by His creation. All benefits emanate from Him, known and unknown. When we experience a goodly outcome from the appropriate action it is a manifestation of the bestower of benefit. Lasting benefit is ultimately the result of seeing the All-Merciful One behind all events and experiences; to witness the one pure light behind all the rainbow colors of the numerous manifestations.

For the illumined believer whatever comes to him will have within it benefit, thus the seeker will always look for Al-Nāfi' even when the outer appearance of an event is affliction.

AL-NŪR
The Light

From *nawwara*: to shine; to shed light; to illuminate; to enlighten. *Nār* is fire, whereas *nūr* is light. Allah describes Himself in the Qur'an as the *Nūr* of the heavens and the earth (24:35). The Prophet *(pbuh)* was described as *nūr*. All creation and life-forms are based on lights (*Anwār*).

Allah is the original absolute Light, and the source of all illumination and creation, which are modified derivatives of His light. His Light includes all invisible lights of knowledge, inspiration and insights. From that pure original divine light comes the paradigm of existential light, shade, and the manifestation of opposites. It is through the experience of dark and shadow that we appreciate and long for eternal light and life, and the light for guidance. The prophets and enlightened beings look at creation through His Light, and discern the perfection behind what appears as confusing or lacking.

When one is in darkness and confusion, call upon Al-Nūr for illumination, guidance, and the ability to witness things as they are. His Light cascades throughout creation and brings about all diversity and multiplicity.

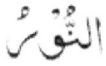

AL-HĀDĪ
The Guide

From *hadā*: to lead in the right way, guide, show; to direct. From the same root comes *hidāyah* or *hudā*: right guidance to what is needed.

Allah is the source of all help and guidance and appropriate action. When His direction and religion are not followed, we travel without a map. It is through His mercy and will that all creation is guided to Him by Him. The more one relies upon, trusts and has faith in Him, the more certain contentment will be the outcome.

Confusion and uncertainty are His early gifts to lead us to the inner serenity and confident contentment of following the commands and lights of Al-Hādī.

AL-BADĪ`
The Originator

From *bada`a*: to produce something new; to originate; to create a novelty.

Allah is the source and origin of all. He began creation and maintains His ever-changing universe without previous models or designs. His infinite varieties of pattern, entities, forms, and shapes float in His cosmos according to His great decrees, maps of movement, and destinies. There was nothing in existence ever, except Him, and all creation are but moving shadows reflecting His Attributes.

When you are looking for creativity and innovation call upon the Al-Badī`.

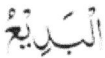

AL-BĀQĪ
The Everlasting

From *baqiya*: to remain, to continue; to be perpetual or permanent. Al-Abqa – the ever-abiding – is also a Divine Name (20:73). Al-Bāqī, the eternally living, appears in the Qur'an in its verbal form (55:27).

Allah is not subject to time and space: thus, Al-Bāqī is the permanent base for all change without involvement in change. He is the Source of ongoingness and the foundation of change and movement. Yearning for longevity is a minor reflection of the everlasting shaft of light called Al-Bāqī. Like all other great Divine Attributes we long for them and thus adore Allah. The entire creation is passionate about permanency, stability, eternity – all of which are His Attributes.

When you experience change, desirable or otherwise, remember that Al-Bāqī is there before and after all events. He is the ultimate reference point.

AL-WĀRITH
The Inheritor

From *waritha*: to revert to; to inherit; to be heir to anyone. Allah is Khayr al-Wārithīn: the Best of Inheritors (21:89). Al-Wārith is inferred from other forms of the word (e.g. 3:180).

As it is He Who will still be there after the end of all creation, He is the true Inheritor. Allah is the creator of all, controls all, maintains all, and thus all belongs to Him from the beginning and after the apparent end. The true just Creator is alone the worthy owner and inheritor. At best we are guests, witnesses, and worshippers with total dependence upon His generosity.

Whenever one is concerned about loss of wealth or possessions, remember the One to Whom everything returns – Al-Wārith – for He is the Creator and proprietor Who has given us a generous loan in this life to lead us to the Garden of the Hereafter.

AL-RASHĪD
The Most Discerning

From the root *rashada*: to follow the right course; to become sensible, mature; to have true faith; to be well guided. *Rashīd* also means discerning. *Rushd* is good sense, proper conduct and integrity. Al-Rashīd appears in the Qur'an describing a virtuous Prophetic quality whose source is a Divine Attribute.

Allah is the source of all maturity, wisdom and discernment. His directions and management are perfect. He is the original Source of all patterns, decrees, and ways which lead towards the arrival at the one ocean of light and eternal peace.

Call upon Al-Rashīd to gain appropriate guidance. Modesty, courage, wisdom, and justice are attributes which relate to *rushd*.

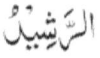

AL-SABŪR
The Patient

From *sabara*: to be patient; to endure; to withstand; to be steadfast and certain.

Allah has created time and space and contains them. Thus He is beyond experiential haste or patience. His patience is absolute: thus, He postpones justice or punishment upon human beings brought on by their errors or transgressions. He delays with clemency and gives numerous opportunities for His creation to discover the way to His presence and grace.

Whenever one experiences impatience hold on to this invocation, for Al-Sabūr enables us to transcend time and perceived difficulty.

AL-RABB
The Lord

The root relates to *rabba*: to grow, increase. *Rabbaba* means to bring up; to be the lord and master of. The *Rabb* of a thing is he who deserves it and possesses it and has power over it. *Tarbiyah* is upbringing, instruction, and grooming.

Allah's mercy and care are behind the force that brings everything up to its full potential and sustains it. Al-Rabb is the most frequently mentioned name in the Qur'an after Allah. Most attributes relate to Al-Rabb, especially those denoting action such as the Creator, the Provider and the Opener. The enlightened being is the reflection of Al-Rabb for what is under his care in this world. The devout parent acts as Rabb to a child and guides their offspring to the real, everlasting Rabb, Allah.

DIVINE NAMES NOT USED IN TIRMIDHI'S/ AL-GHAZALI'S LISTS

Al-Hafī – *The Gracious, Kind One*

From the root *hafiya*: to honor greatly; to be gracious and kind.

The Lord of creation loves what He creates and welcomes all creation to His divine dominion.

Al-Qarīb – *The Near One*

From the root *qaruba*: to approach; to be near, close; to have a relationship, affinity.

Allah permeates and engulfs all of His creation. He is therefore nearer than nearness itself.

Al-Ghālib – *The One Who Prevails, Overcomes*

From the root *ghalaba*: to overcome; to prevail; to be victorious; to master; to conquer.

Allah is the everlasting Reality and therefore nothing can prevail over Him.

Al-Fātir – *The Splitter*

From the root *fatara*: to split apart; to render asunder; to create (from nothing). *Fitrah* means primal pattern.

The cosmos emanates from the void of pre-creation. All manifestations originate when the seeds, which bear their design, are cracked or split open.

Al-Khallāq – *The Creative Creator*

From the root *khalaqa*: to measure accurately; to define the dimensions of anything; to create and produce; to fashion or mold.

Allah has designed His creation in an infinite variety of sizes, colors and attributes. Contemplating creation can be an act of adoring the Creator.

Al-Khayr – *The Good*

From the root *khāra* the following meanings are derived: to do good; to bless; to choose (well); to prefer.

Allah's design and intention are both based on His mercy and goodwill; therefore He expects the best outcome for His creation.

Al-Kāfī – *The All-Sufficient*

From the root *kafā*: to suffice, be enough; to be satisfied, to remain contented.

Allah is sufficient unto Himself and to His creation. The more we become aware of Allah's ways, the more content we become.

Al-Muhīt – *The All-Encompassing One*

From the root *hāta*: to guard; to surround; to encompass; to comprehend.

The creative essence permeates all creation and that is how all gross and subtle realities connect and interlink.

Al-Mubīn – *The Evident One*

From the root *bana*: to be distinct and separate.

Allah encompasses physical creation, its meaning, attributes, and the sources from which it emanates. It is thus that the Creator is evident in different formats.

Al-Mawlā – *The Master*

From the root *waliya*: to be near, to be master of, to have power.

The Creator is ever-present and accessible in all His creation.

Al-Musta`ān – *The One Whose Aid is to Be Implored*

From the root `āwana`: to assist; to Help one another and *ista`āna*, to ask for help.

No power or life is independent of its Source. Thus true reliance is upon Allah for He is the source of all help.

Al-Nāsir – *The Giver Of Victory*

From the root *nasara*: to assist, help; to protect; to deliver.

Victory is based on achievement and life. Nothing can be accomplished unless it is according to Allah's decrees and laws. Victory is only by Allah. The ultimate victory is to be with Him without seeing other than Him.

COMPOUND NAMES

Dhū al-'Arsh – *Possesser of the Throne*

Dhū al-Tawl – *Possessor of Superabundance*

Dhū al-Ma`ārij – *The Lord of Ascension*

Rafī`al-Darajāt – *Possesor of Exalted Ranks (Qualities)*

Sarī` al-`Iqāb – *The Swift in Punishment*

Shadid al-`Iqab – *The Severe in Punishment*

Shadīd al-Mihāl – *The Inexorable in His Will*

Fāliq al-Isbāh – *The Splitter of Dawn*

Fāliq al-Habb wa wa al-Nuwa – *The Splitter of Seeds and Kernels*

Khayr al-Munzilīn – *The Best of Those Who Bring Down*

Khayr al-Mākirīn – *The Best of Planners*

Khayr al-Fāsilīn – *The Best of Differentiators*

Ahl al-Maghfirah – *The Worthy of Being Forgiving*

Ahl al-*Taqwā* – *The Worthy of Being Regarded with Cautious Awareness*

Ahsan al-Khāliqīn – *The Best of Creators*

Al-Rahmān Al-Rahīm – *The Beneficent, the Most Merciful*

Ahkamu al-Hākimīn – *The Wisest of Judges*

Al-Qā'im 'Alā kulli nafsin bimā kasabat – *He Who Observes what every self earns*

**Al-`Ālim al-Ghayb** – *The Knower of all unknown.* Other variations: `Alām al-Ghuyūb, and `Alīm al-Ghayb wa al-Shahādah.

PART III
ADDITIONS

INTRODUCTION

This part includes four sections: the first is a selection of relevant Qur'anic *āyāt*; the second presents relevant Prophetic teachings; the third offers some special invocations and *du`ā*; and the fourth section contains a glossary of essential terms.

The brief selection of Qur'anic *āyāt* have been referred to in the text, especially in part one. Several of these *āyāt* are special invocations and are often used by Muslims in their devotions.

There is no special order in the listing of these *āyāt*. As for their translation, I have endeavored to bring out the inner spirit and meaning without impairing correctness of translation.

As for the Prophetic teachings, the list is very brief and most have already been referred to in different parts of the text. This selection does not include any weak or controversial sayings, and they are easily traceable from popular books and serious scholarly works.

The *du'ā*'s included are from several popular Muslim compilations, that can be traced back to Islam Original and the Prophetic tradition.

The glossary of terms is mostly a selection of important relevant terms worthy of being studied and learnt, for without them one will not have access to the depths of the *Dīn*. As the meanings of the Divine Names have been elaborated upon within the text of the book, they have not been included here.

The emphasis in this presentation has been brevity and ease of use as well as relevance for the contemporary Muslim. I have deliberately refrained from including a reading list, as books on Islam are multiplying in subject and flavor and in ever-increasing languages. Although the *kufr* system now prevails globally, so does access to His Ever Present Light through sincere submission, *īmān* and *tawhīd*.

I pray to Allah to maintain awareness of His Ever-Presence to enable us to lift the veils and barriers of the self and mental illusions. There will be no spiritual progress and illumination save for His unconditional mercy and *rahmah*.

RELEVANT AYATS FROM THE QUR'AN

And Allah's is the unseen in the heavens and the earth, and to Him the whole affair will be returned.
So serve Him and put thy trust in Him.
And thy Lord is not heedless of what you do.
(11:123)

Our Lord, I have settled a part of my offspring in a valley unproductive of fruit near Thy Sacred House, our Lord, that they may keep up prayer; so make the hearts of some people yearn towards them, and provide them with fruits; haply they may be grateful.
(14:37)

And man prays for evil as he ought to pray for good;
And man is ever hasty.
(17:11)

Say: Call on Allah or call on the Beneficent. By whatever (Name) you call on Him, He has the best names. And utter not thy prayer loudly nor be silent in it,
and seek a way between these.
(17:110)

Allah – there is no God but He. His are the most beautiful names.
(20:8)

And when Abraham said: My Lord, make this a secure town and provide its people with fruits, such of them as believe in Allah and the Last Day. He said: And whoever disbelieves, I shall grant him enjoyment for a short while, then I shall drive him to the chastisement of the Fire. And it is an evil destination.
(2:126)

And when my servants ask thee concerning Me, surely I am nigh. I answer the prayer of the supplicant when he calls on Me, so they should hear My call and believe in Me that they may walk in the right way.
(2:186)

Or, Who answers the distressed one when he calls upon Him and removes the evil, and will make you successors in the earth? Is there a God with Allah? Little is it that you mind!
(27:62)

And when harm afflicts men, they call upon their Lord, turning to Him, then when He makes them taste of mercy from Him, lo! some of them begin to associate (others) with their Lord,
(30:33)

So their Lord accepted their prayer, (saying): I will not suffer the work of any worker among you to be lost whether male or female, the one of you being from the other. So those who fled and were driven forth from their homes and persecuted in My way and who fought and were slain, I shall truly remove their evil and make them enter Gardens wherein flow rivers – a reward from Allah. And with Allah is the best reward.
(3:195)

O you who believe, remember Allah with much remembrance,
(33.41)

And your Lord says: Pray to Me, I will answer you. Those who disdain My service will surely enter hell, abased.
(40:60)

And that man can have nothing but what he strives for:
(53:39)

And that his striving will soon be seen.
(53:40)

He is Allah, besides Whom there is no God; The King, the Holy, the Author of Peace, the Granter of Security, Guardian over all, the Mighty, the Supreme, the Possessor of greatness. Glory be to Allah from that which they set up (with Him)!
(59:23)

He is Allah, the Creator, the Maker, the Fashioner: His are the most beautiful names. Whatever is in the heavens and the earth declares His glory; and He is the Mighty, the Wise.
(59:24)

And gives him sustenance from whence he imagines not. And whoever trusts in Allah, He is sufficient for him. Surely Allah attains His purpose. Allah indeed has appointed a measure for everything.
(65:3)

And Allah's are the best names, so call on Him thereby and leave alone those who violate the sanctity of His names. They will be recompensed for what they do.
(7:180)

And remember thy Lord within thyself humbly and fearing, and in a voice not loud, in the morning and the evening, and be not of the heedless.
(7:205)

They said: Our Lord, we have wronged ourselves; and if Thou forgive us not, and have (not) mercy on us, we shall certainly be of the losers.
(7:23)

RELEVANT PROPHETIC TEACHINGS

- Whoever is preoccupied in remembering Me from asking Me, I shall grant him the best of what is given to those who ask.
- Supplication is the weapon of the believer.
- Supplication is the brain of worship and no one perishes with it.
- He who knows Allah most will ask Him most.
- If you wish to ask Allah something and be given it, then despair from [asking] all people.
- Do not despise the call of anyone because even Jews and Christians are answered.
- If an entire people have gathered to benefit you in something, they will not benefit you, except in that which is written for you, and if they have gathered to harm you with something, nothing will come to you except that which is written for you. The pens are withdrawn and the sheets are dry.
- They asked *Imam* Ja`far al-Sadiq, 'We call and are not answered'. He said, 'Because you are asking whom you do not know.'

The Prophet (*pbuh*) recommended the following *du`a* to be recited, when asking for anything or an opening:

Lā ilāha illā Allah wahdahu lā sharīka lahu.

Lahu al-mulk wa lahu al-hamd wa huwa 'Alā kulli shay'in qadīr.
Lā ilāha illā Allah wa lā hawlah wa lā quwwata illā billāh.

The Prophet (*pbuh*) also said: 'No Muslim calls the supplication of Yunus, when he was in the belly of the whale, but that Allah accepts it':
Lā ilāha illā anta subhānaka innī kuntu min al-zālimīn.

The Prophet (*pbuh*) said that this *du`ā* was especially for Yunus, and the answer is in the Qur'an: 'and We saved him from his grief', and that is how Allah will save the believer.

Throughout the history of Muslim scholars and the enlightened ones, there has been a debate as to which is the *Ism al-A`dham*. There are several dozens of recommendations, prominent among them being Al-Hayyu Al-Qayyūm. The Prophetic tradition says:

Allahu lā ilāha illā anta al-Ahad al-Samad al-ladhī lam yalid wa lam yūlad
wa lam yakun lahu kufu'an ahad.

When somebody calls the following *du'ā*, the Prophet (*pbuh*) said that he has called the Greatest Name, and that he will be answered:

O Compassionate, O Munificent, O Innovator Of the heavens and the earth, O Master of Majesty and Nobility!

Yā Hannān yā Mannān yā Badī' al-samawāti wa al-ard yā Dhū al-Jalāli wa al-Ikrām.

Another great supplication attributed to the Prophet (*pbuh*) is:

> I ask you by every Name that belongs to You and by which You called yourself or which has descended in Your Book or has been taught to any of Your Creation or has been kept in the unseen Knowledge with you.

The Prophet's (*pbuh*) teachings and traditions are numerous in respect to reciting and calling upon Allah's Names and Attributes. One such is his teaching to his daughter Fatima to recite every morning and evening:

> O Ever-Living, O Eternal (Ya Hayyu Ya Qayyūm), I cling to Your Mercy. Render all my affairs good, and do not let me depend upon myself even for and instant.

Divine Names and Attributes are all desirable and sought after by Creation and some of them are totally unique to the Creator. Some Names and Attributes can also be an attribute of Creation, but only to a limited degree, such as what is considered the Seven Key Names, *Al-`Alīm, Al-Basīr, Al-Hayy, Al-Murīd, Al-Muttakallim, Al-Samī`* and *Al-Qadīr*. These Seven Key Names are to do with the Attributes of knowledge, seeing, life, the ability to learn, talking, hearing and the ability to will.

It is related from the *Imam*s of the family of the Prophet (*pbuh*) that:

- Whoever reads Surat al-Nabā' daily, a year will not pass before he will be invited by Allah to go to Makkah.
- Whoever reads Surat al-Tīn, Allah will collect for him all the goodness of the *dunyā* and the

ākhirah.

- Whoever reads Surat al-Nazi`at will not enter the garden except as one who is completely fulfilled, and will not have any *shaqā'* (suffering or misery) in this *dunyā*.
- Whoever reads Surat al-Burūj over water and then drinks that water after any poison he has taken, he will be cured of that poison.
- Whoever reads Surat al-Qadr in every obligatory prayer, a caller will call: "O slave of Allah, all your past actions have been forgiven, now carry on with your good actions."
- If one among you has a severe headache or some similar pain, he should spread his hands out and read Surat al-Fātihah, Surat al-Ikhlās, and the last two Surahs of the Qur'an, and should then wipe his hands on his forehead seeking relief from the headache.
- Whoever goes to his bed and reads Surat al-Ikhlās eleven times, his dwelling will be safe and all those areas surrounding him will also be kept safe.
- Whoever reads Surat al-Zilzāl four times, it is as though he has read the entire Qur'an.

Allah has revealed to the Prophet (*pbuh*) by saying (*Hadīth Qudsi*):

> There is between Me and human beings and jinn a most serious matter.
> I create and other than Me is worshipped.
> I provide and other than Me is thanked.
> My Goodness and Grace descends upon all My Creation, whilst their evil rises up to Me.

I get close to them Lovingly with my Bounty, and they turn away from Me with their disobedience.

I am rich beyond any means, and they are the poor ones in constant need.

Those who are in constant remembrance of Me truly receive My Love, and those who are in true gratitude of Me will experience increase.

Yet, I do not deprive My enemies from My mercy. A good deed for Me I return ten-fold and more.

An evil deed will be reciprocated to the same extent of it, and I still forgive My Creation.

I am gentler with My Creation than a mother with her newborn.

FEW SPECIAL *DU`A*

Following are some special *du`ā* from the Qur'an and from collections of Hadīth:

Du`ā Nūr as related by the Prophet (*pbuh*):

In the Name of Allah, Light upon Light. In the Name of Allah, the Arranger of all affairs, Who created Light from Light and brought down Light upon the Tūr (Sinai) in a written book, in a sheet that is spread in a measure that is predetermined, upon a Prophet chosen.

Praise be to He, Who is gloriously remembered and in honor famous, and in ease and difficulty thanked. And Allah pray on his progeny and his family.

> *Allah imposes not on any soul a duty beyond its scope. For it is that which it earns (of good and against it that which it works (of evil). Our Lord, punish us not if we forget or make a mistake. Our Lord, do not lay on us a burden as Thou didst lay on those before us. Our Lord, impose not on us (afflictions) which we have not the strength to bear.*
>
> *And pardon us! And grant us protection! And have mercy on us! Thou art our Patron, so grant us victory over the disbelieving people. (2:286)*

And there are some among them who say:

> "Our Lord, grant us good in this world and good in the Hereafter, and save us from the chastisement of the Fire."
> (2:201)

> Our Lord, grant me protection and my parents and the believers on the day when the reckoning comes to pass.
> (14:41)

The following is a highly rewarded *du`ā* according to Muslim:

Glory be to Allah and grace is His (as great as) the number of His creatures, the extent of His satisfaction, the weight of His domain, and the ink (needed to write down His countless) signs (of presence, omnipotence, and grace).

The Prophet (*pbuh*) called the following *du`ā*, 'The Master *Du`ā* for seeking forgiveness', according to Al-Bukhari. It should be recited three times:

Oh Allah! You are my Lord, there is no deity but You. You created me and I am Your slave-servant. And I am trying my best to keep my oath (of faith) to You and to seek to live in the hope of Your promise. I seek refuge in You from my greatest-evil deeds. I acknowledge Your blessings upon me and I acknowledge my sins. So forgive me, for none but You can forgive sins.

According to Abu Daud, Al-Tirmidhi, and Al-Nisa`i, to

recite Surat al-Ikhlās, Surat al-Falaq, and Surat al-Nās three times each in the morning and evening is highly recommended (for protection).

Salāt al-Hājah is the prayer and supplication of one who is in need: Perform *wudu* in the best of manners and offer two *rak`āt* of *Salāt al-Hājah*. Praise Allah and recite *Durūd*. Thereafter, recite the following *Du`ā*:

> *There is no deity besides Allah, the Most Forbearing and Kind, who is unblemished and Lord of the Great Throne, so praise be to Allah, the Cherisher of the worlds.*
>
> *I do seek all causes of the grant of Your mercy and forgiveness, and I do seek thorough escape from sin, a full share of virtuous deeds and complete safety from inequity.*
>
> *(Oh Allah,) Let not a single sin of mine be left out from being forgiven, nor worry and pain from being relieved, nor need which is agreeable to You from being fulfilled,*
> *O You Most Merciful and Compassionate.*

Recitation of the following *du`ā* seven times in the morning and in the evening is recommended by the Prophet (*pbuh*) as a means of seeking the protection of Allah from anything which is worrying us:

> But if they turn away, say:
>
> *Allah is sufficient for me – there is no God but He. On Him do I rely, and He is the Lord of the mighty Throne. (9:129)*

SELECTED PART OF THE HAYDARI WIRD (LITANY)

Oh Allah, truly, I ask You by
Your Name, Allah, the All-merciful,
The All-compassionate.
Oh Possessor of majesty and splendour!
Oh Living! Oh Self-subsistent!
Oh You Whom there is no God but You!
Oh He! Oh He Whom none knows what

He is,
nor How He is,
nor where He is,
nor in what respect He is but He!

Oh Possessor of the dominion and the kingdom!
Oh Possessor of might and invincibility!
Oh King! Oh All-sacred!
Oh All-peaceable!
Oh All-faithful!
Oh All-preserver! Oh All-mighty!
Oh All-compeller!
Oh All-sublime! Oh Creator! Oh Maker!
Oh Shaper!
Oh Benefiter! Oh Director! Oh Severe!
Oh Originator!
Oh Returner! Oh Destroyer!
Oh All-loving!

Oh All-praiseworthy! Oh All-worshipful!
Oh Far!
Oh Near!
Oh Responder! Oh Watcher!
Oh Reckoner!
Oh Innovator!
Oh Exalter! Oh Inaccessible!
Oh All-hearing! Oh All-knowing!
Oh All-clement! Oh All-generous!
Oh All-wise! Oh Eternal! Oh All-high!
Oh All-tremendous! Oh All-comforting!
Oh All-gracious! Oh Accounter!
Oh Recourse! Oh All-majestic!
Oh All-beautiful! Oh Guardian!
Oh Surety! Oh Annuller! Oh Obtainer!
Oh All-noble! Oh Leader! Oh Guide!
Oh All-apparent! Oh First! Oh Last!
Oh Outward! Oh Inward!
Oh All-steadfast! Oh Everlasting!
Oh Knower! Oh Decider! Oh Judge!
Oh Just! Oh Separator! Oh Joiner!
Oh Pure! Oh Purifier! Oh All-powerful!
Oh All-able! Oh All-great!
Oh All-sublime! Oh One! Oh Unique!

Oh Everlasting Refuge!
Oh He Who begets not and was not begotten,
and equal to Whom there is none!
Oh He Who is exalted and dominates!
Oh He Who is master and exercises power!
Oh He Who is inward and aware!
Oh He Who is worshipped and thankful!
Oh He Who is disobeyed and forgives!
Oh He Who is not encompassed by thoughts,

nor perceived by vision and from
Whom no trace remains hidden!
Oh Provider of mankind!
Oh Determiner of every lot!
Oh Lofty of place!
Oh Firm in supports!
Oh Transformer of Time!
Oh Acceptor of sacrifices!
Oh Possessor of graciousness and benevolence!
Oh Possessor of might and force!
Oh All-compassionate!
Oh All-merciful!

Oh He Who is every day upon some labour!
Oh He Who is not distracted from one labour by another!
Oh Tremendous in rank!
Oh He Who is in every place!
Oh He Who Hears all sounds!
Oh He Who answers all supplications!
Oh He Who fulfils all entreaties!
Oh He Who provides all needs!
Oh He Who sends down blessings!
Oh He Who has mercy upon tears!
Oh He Who cancels out false steps!
Oh He Who removes troubles!
Oh He Who sponsors good things!
Oh He Who exalts in rank!
Oh He Who bestows requests!
Oh He Who gives life to the dead!
Oh He Who gathers all scattered things!
Oh He Who is aware of all intentions!
Oh He Who brings back what has passed away!
Oh Most Munificent of the most munificent!
Oh Most Generous of the most generous!

Oh Helper of those who seek aid!
Oh Goal of the seekers!
Oh Lord! Oh Lord! Oh Lord!
Oh All-generous! Oh All-generous!
Oh All-generous!

By Your mercy, Oh Most Merciful of the merciful!

GLOSSARY OF TERMS

As the meanings of most of the Divine Names have been presented in the main text, they have not been replicated here. This glossary is based on an earlier version published by Zahra Publications, so the terms are of interest to the serious student and do not relate only to this present work. Large Roman numerals after some root verbs indicate verbal forms for those who wish to know. An apostrophe at the beginning of a word beginning with 'a' 'i' or 'u' signifies the letter `ayn, (pronounced from the throat). When an apostrophe appears in the middle or at the end of a word it could either be `ayn or the *hamza* (glottal stop).

> *Allāh* – God; the greatest Name of God. Literally 'the God'. Allah designates the Source from which all things seen and unseen emanate and return. The name encompasses all the Divine Names (also known as the Most Beautiful Names of Allah) such as **al-Awwal** (the First), **al-Ākhir** (the Last), **al-Zāhir** (the Manifest), **al-Bātin** (the Hidden).

> `*Abd* – Servant; worshipper or slave (of Allah); also human being, man. From the root `abada, to serve, worship. Derivatives: `ibādah, worship, adoration, i.e. obeying Allah in humility

and service and holding fast to the *Dīn* (qv.); **`ubūdīyyah**, servitude or obedience to Allah defined by being faithful to the contract (between man and Allah), observing the limits, being content with what there is and forbearing when what was there has passed or been lost.

*`Adl* – Equity, justice rectitude, fairness, honesty. From `**adala** (I), to act justly, equitably; `**addala** (II) to straighten, set in order; `**ādala** (III), to be equal. An `ādil is someone who is just, fair, equitable, upright. Divine Name: **al-`Adl**, the Just, i.e. He Whom desire does not cause to incline or decline so that He should deviate from the right course.

Ākhirah – The Hereafter, the latter or last life, the abode of everlasting duration. Opposite of **dunyā** (qv.). From **akhkhara** (II) to delay, put off, defer, postpone. Derivatives: **ākhir**, another, other (e.g. other than the former or first, as in 'another man'); Divine Name: **al-Ākhir**, the Last, or He who remains after all creatures and Creation perish.

*`Aql* – Faculty of reason, intellect, discernment, rationality, mind. From `**aqala**, to keep back (a camel by tying its foreleg), to confine, to be restricted, to be reasonable, to understand. True reason and intelligence can only be exercised by keeping the lower self (qv. **nafs**) tethered.

Ard – The earth, land, a country, soil (as distinct from **dunyā**, the world as we experience it).

*`Azm* – Determination, firm will, resolution; as in **ūlū' al-`azm**: those apostles possessed of resolution (46:35). From `**azama**, to be patient,

to determine, resolve, decide upon (doing something).

Āyah – pl. āyāt. Verse from the Qur'an; sign or mark.

Balā' – Trial, tribulation, affliction, misfortune; also, bravery, gallantry. From **balā**, to try, put to the test. **Balā'** follows **fanā'** (qv.) in order to purify and re-educate the slave in his new situation through trial and precedes **baqā'** (qv.).

Baqa' – Going on in Allah (see **fanā'** and **balā'**); remaining, continuing; continuation of existence after this life, eternal life. From the root **baqiya**, to continue. Divine Name: **al-Bāqī**, the Evercontinuing, He Whose existence has no end.

Basīrah – Keen insight (as opposed to outward vision), discernment, understanding, power of mental perception. From **basara**, to look, see, realize, comprehend.

Bātil – False, untrue, vain, futile, unfounded, useless. Opposite of **haqq** (qv.) From **batala** (I), to be or become null, void, false, worthless; to be devoid of virtue or efficacy; to become obsolete. **Battala** (II), to thwart, foil, neutralize; **abtala** (IV) like II, also to speak what is false, make vain claims, prattle.

Bushrā – Glad tidings, good news which causes the complexion of the person to whom the news is announced to change. From **bashira** (I), to rejoice, be delighted, happy; to peel, to scrape (the skin on which hair grows); **bashshara** (II) to announce or spread good news. Derivatives: **bishārah**, good news, annunciation; **bashīr**, bringer of glad tidings, messenger, herald; **bashar**, human being (thus called because the human skin is bare of hair or wool).

Birr – Reverence, piety, righteousness. From root **barra**, to act justly, to be reverent, dutiful, devoted, to obey.

Dhanb – (pl. **Dhūnūb**) misdeed, offence, sin, crime, act of disobedience, transgression (whether intentional or unintentional; a purely intentional misdeed is called **ithm**). From **dhanaba** (I), to follow closely, to follow one's tail (said of an animal); **dhannaba** (II) (of a locust) to stick its tail in the ground to lay eggs, (of dates) to ripen; **adhnaba** (IV) to commit a crime or fault. Derivative: **dhanab**, tail.

Dhikr – Remembrance of Allah, stimulated by the invocation of His Divine Names and other formulae from the Qur'an and sayings of the Prophet (*pbuh*). From **dhakara**, to remember, think, relate; to strike a man on his private parts. Derivatives: **tadhkirah**, warning, admonition, recollection; **dhakar**, male. (See **insān** re: man's forgetfulness and need to be reminded).

Dīn – Life-transaction. Usually translated as religion which does not trans–mit full significance of term. **Dīn** is the transaction between the debtor (Allah) and the indebted (man). From the root **dāna**, to owe, be indebted to, take a loan, be inferior. Hence living the **Dīn** means repaying one's debt to the Creator in a manner that befits the potential high station of man in creation.

*Du`ā'* – Act of seeking, desiring, asking, demanding, supplicating Allah. From **da`ā** to call, summon, appeal, invite, invoke. Derivatives: **dā`ī**, one who invites or calls to Allah; **da`wā**, claim, allegation; **da`wah**, call, appeal, incitation to Allah.

Dunyā – This world (as opposed to the Next life, **ākhirah** qv.); wordly, temporal things or possessions. **Dunyā** is rendered real by attachment to it. From **dāna**, to be low or near; to be base or vile. Derivatives: **adnā** worse, baser, viler; **hayāt al-dunyā**, the life of this world (baser then the life of the Next, for here the gross prevails over the subtle. Thus in this world **sharī`ah** (qv.) prevails over **haqīqah** (qv.), for its obligations must be fulfilled first).

Fanā' – Annihilation in Allah; passing away, vanishing, cessation of being. The Prophet (*pbuh*) said: 'Die before you die.' **Fanā'** is death in meaning based on the cessation of attributes. It is a climactic experience which is followed by **balā'** and **baqā'** (qv.). From **faniya**, to pass away, to cease to exist, to wane, be spent. **Dār al-fanā'** is the abode of transitoriness, i.e. the present world.

Fārigh – Free, empty, unoccupied. From **faragha**, to be empty, vacant; to be done, finished, and **farigha**, to be free from any occupation (qv. 28:10, 94:7).

Fasād – Acting corruptly, corruption, violence. From **fasada**, to be corrupt. He who acts in this manner is a **mufsid** (pl. *mufsidun, mufsidin*).

Fikr – Reflection, meditation, contemplation. From the root **fakara**, to reflect, ponder, cogitate, think. Creation is full of signs for those who '*yatafakkarun*', i.e. reflect.

Fiqh – Understanding, comprehension, knowledge; has come to specifically refer to Islamic jurisprudence. From **faqaha**, to be superior in wisdom, and **faqiha** to be wise, to be skilled in matters pertaining to law **tafaqqaha** (V) is to be assiduous in instructing oneself.

Fitnah – Temptation, trial, enchantment, seduction, captivation; a burning with fire (melting gold and silver in order to separate the bad from the good). **Fitnah** is whatever distracts or disturbs, thus it also means riot and civil strife. The purpose of **fitnah** is to show the true nature of what is being afflicted. From the verb **fatana** (I) to turn away (from s.o.), to try, tempt, seduce; **fattana** (II) to enamour, charm, enthrall, infatuate. A **dinar maftūn** is a coin, proven to be real gold or silver.

Fitrah – Man's natural disposition, his innate nature, the human blueprint, the natural constitution with which a child is created in the mother's womb; also, Creation, the bringing into existence. From **fatara** (I), to split, to cleave the flesh and come forth, to originate, create; **aftara** (IV) to break fast; **infatara** (VII) to become, cracked open (82:1). Derivatives: **futūr**, fissure; **fatūr**, breakfast; **iftār**, breaking of fast at sunset; **infitār**, cleaving asunder. See Qur'an 30:29.

Fu'ād – The heart. Synonymous with **qalb** (qv.) but whereas latter evokes image of turning on its own axis like a radar sweep, **fu'ād** pulsates and lends faculty of sharpness to the mind or intellect (cf. 53:2), i.e. it does not lie. From **fa'ada** (I), to hurt s.o. in the heart and **tafa`ada** (V), to be excited with ardour, to be in a state of motion. See 28:10.

Furqān – Application of discrimination, discernment to distinguish between falsehood and truth. Thus it is also an epithet of the Qur'an. From **faraqa**, to split, divide, make a distinction.

Ghadab – Wrath, anger, fury. From **ghadiba** (I) to be angry, furious; to stand up and defend. **Aghdaba** (IV) to annoy, enrage. **Maghdūb** (cf. Surat al-Fatihah), object of anger.

Ghayb – Realms of the Unseen; whatever is absent or hidden. From **ghaba**(I), to be distant, remote, absent, hidden; to be beyond reach or perception by the senses; **ightāba** (VIII) to speak evil of someone in their absence, hence **ghībah** means backbiting or slander.

Ghurūr – Deception, delusion; conceit; vanities; danger. From **gharra** (I), to deceive, beguile, mislead; to make one desire what is vain or false; **gharrara** (II), to delude, dazzle, entice; expose to danger, jeopardize.

Hajj – Pilgrimage (in the last month of Islamic calendar year). From **hajja** (I), to betake oneself towards an object of veneration, to respect, honour; **hajjaja** (II) to overcome, defeat (with arguments and evidence), to convince, to make pilgrimage to Makkah; **hāajaja** (III) to dispute, debate, reason. Derivatives: **hujjah**, proof, evidence, hence authoritative source; **hajji**, a pilgrim, honorific title of one who has performed pilgrimage.

Hamd – Praise, laudation. From **hamida**, to praise, extol. **Al-hamdu li'Llah** means praise belongs to Allah. By reciting this phrase one is not giving praise to Allah, for it is already His; therefore, to correctly express gratitude it is recited in conjunction with **shukruli'Llah** (qv. **shukr**), which is from the slave to the Lord. **Mahmūd**, praised; **Ahmad**, most praiseworthy; **Muhammad**, most praised; Divine Name: **al-Hamīd**, the Most Praised. **Sūrat al-Fātihah** is also known as **Sūrat al-Hamd**, the Chapter of Praise.

Haqīqah – Inner reality, truth, science of the inward; the realm of meaning as opposed to **sharī'ah** (qv.), the realm of senses. See also **tarīqah** to understand this triad of terms. From **haqqa** (I) to be true, right, just, authentic, valid; and **haqqaqa** (II) to realize, make something come true. Divine Name: **al-Haqq**, the Truth, Whose being is never changed.

Hayāt – Life, life-blood, liveliness. From **hayya**, to live, experience. Divine Name: **al-Hayy**, the Everliving.

Hijrah Departure, exodus, emigration. Year of **Hijrah** (622 AD) when Prophet (*pbuh*) had to leave Makkah for Madinah. From **hajara**, to disassociate, separate; renounce, avoid, abandon, relinquish.

Hubb – Love, affection. From **habba** (I) to love, like; to become loved, liked, approved; **habbaba** (II) to evoke love endear, produce seed (of plant), granulate; **ishtahabba** (X), to like or deem desirable, recommendable, to prefer. Derivatives: **habb**, grains, seed; **mustahabb**, recommended act whose neglect is not punished but whose performance is rewarded.

Hudā – Right guidance, way or direction. From **hadā**, to lead in the right way. Derivatives: **mahdī**, rightly guided; **hidāyah**, guidance; **hadīyyah**, gift; Divine Name: **al-Hādī**, the Rightly Guiding, Who guides His slaves to knowledge of Him.

Iblīs – A name of Satan; the Jinn who out of arrogance disobeyed Allah's command to prostrate before Adam. From **ablasa**, to despair; give up hope (of the mercy of Allah).

Ihsān – Performance of good deeds, excellence, beneficence. The culmination of the progression from **islām** (qv.) to **īmān** (qv.) to the state of 'though one does not see Allah one acts in full certainty that He sees oneself'. From **ahsana** (IV), to act well, pleasingly, expertly, to do good; **hasuna** (I) to be or become handsome, beautiful, good, to be in a desirable condition. Derivatives: **husn**, beauty; **muhsin**, person in state of **ihsān**, beneficent, charitable; **Hasan, Husayn**, excellent, beautiful; **asmā' al-husnā**, the Most Beautiful Names of Allah (the Ninety Nine Divine Names).

Ikhlās – Pure sincerity. From **khalasa** (I), to be pure and sincere, to be clear, free of admixture, and **akhlasa** (IV) to clarify, to be sincere (to Allah) without hypocrisy. **Khulāsah**, clarified butter. See Surat Ikhlas.

*`Ilm* – Knowledge, learning, certainty. From **`alima**, to know, be cognizant, aware. Divine Name: **al-`Alīm**, the Omniscient.

Īmān – Faith, trust, belief, acceptance. From **amana** (I), to believe and **amina**, to be tranquil in heart and mind, to become safe or secure, to trust; **āmana** (IV), to render secure, grant safety. Īmān is being true to the trust with respect to which Allah has confided in one by a firm, believing of the heart, not by professing it on the tongue only. Derivatives: **amn**, peace, security, protection (the opposite of **khawf**); **amīn**, trustworthy, faithful, honest – designation of the Prophet (*pbuh*); **mu'min**, a believer, he who is given certainty and trust; Divine Name: **al-Amīn**, He Who is secure from any causality.

Insān – Man, human being. Opposite of being wild. From the root **anisa**, to be companionable, sociable, friendly. Derivatives: **insānīyyah**, humanity or humanness; **musta'nas**, tame; **uns**, intimacy with Allah. According to one source **insān** is related to **nasiya**, meaning to forget: man had been entrusted with authority. He forgets to honour it and therefore must be reminded. **Insān al-kāmil**, the perfect, complete, man. **Insān al-Kabīr**, literally, the greater man, is the whole of creation.

`Iqāb` – Punishment, penalty, from `aqaba` (I), to strike on the heel, to succeed; `aqqaba` (II), to retrace one's steps. Derivatives: `uqb`, success; `āqibah`, end result.

Iqāmah – Raising, lifting up, elevation; second call to stand ready for prayer. From **qāma** (I) to stand still in one place, to get up, stand erect, pass (as in spend time); to undertake; to be situated. **Istaqāma** (X) to rise, straighten up; be right, correct, sound. Derivatives: **qiyāmah**, resurrection (**yawm al-qiyāmah**: the Day of Resurrection); **qawm**, a body of people composing a community; **mustaqīm**, up-right, straight, correct, harmonious; **maqām**, literally 'the place of the feet', site, location, station (e.g. **maqām al-ihsān**, qv.); **qayyim**, valuable, precious (6:162, 9:36).

Islam – Submission (to the Will of Allah). From **aslama** (IV) to submit, commit (oneself); **salama** (I), to be safe and sound, unimpaired, intact, blameless, to be free; **sallama** (II), to preserve, to deliver, hand over, salute. The **Muslim** is he who trusts in and submits to Allah. Islam comes before full faith and certainty can take root, i.e. **īmān** (qv.), which then transforms the active state of the slave into that of **ihsān** (qv.).

Isrāf – Extravagance, intemperance, prodigality. From **asrafa** (IV), to exceed all bounds, be immoderate, extravagant, squander, dissipate. The **musrif** is he who is immoderate, excessive and wasteful.

Istighfār – Seeking of forgiveness from Allah. From **astaghfara** (X), to seek forgiveness, pardon, to ask for the effects of one's faults to be covered; **ghafara** (I) to cover over. Derivatives: **ghufrān**, forgiveness; Divine Name: **al-Ghafūr**, the most Forgiving.

Jahannam – Hell or hell-fire; the abode of punishment. **Jahannam** is the fire of the next world because of its depth. **Jahnīm** is a bottomless pit.

Jannah – Garden, Paradise. From **janna** (I), to cover, hide, conceal, veil, become dark. Derivatives: **jinn**, invisible entitles made of smokeless fire (as opposed to the clay of Adam and the light of the Angels); **junūn**, possession, madness, insanity; **majnūn**, mad, obsessed; **janīn**, embryo.

Jihād – Exertion of one's utmost power and effort in contending with an object of disapproval; fight, battle in the way of Allah. From **jahada** (I), to endeavour, strive, or labour diligently; **jāhada** (III), to fight for something; **ajhada** (IV), to strain, exert, wear out. **Ijtihād** means effort, pains, utmost application, diligence in reaching legal judgements; **mujtahid** is diligent, industrious, a legist; **mujāhid** is a warrior, fighter.

Kadh – Exertion, toil, labor. From **kadaha**, to work hard.

Kashf – Uncovering, unveiling, revelation, illumination. From **kashafa**, to pull away, remove (a covering or veil), reveal, shed light.

Kayd – Plan, ruse, stratagem, artful device (by which one is taken unaware). From **kāda**, to struggle to manage something, to deceive, beguile, circumvent, outwit.

Khawf – Fear, dread. Conjunct of **rajā'** (qv.). From **Khāfa** (I), to fear, dread, or apprehend something; **khawwafa** (II), to terrify. When **khawf** is realized and harmonized within the self it becomes *taqwā* (qv.)

Khusr – Loss, damage. From **khasira**, to incur a loss, suffer damage, go astray. **Khusrān** is a state of loss, or of being deceived or cheated.

Kufr – Denial and rejection (of the existence of Allah); unbelief, ingratitude. From **kafara**, to cover, hide, be ungrateful, not to believe. The **kāfir** denies the existence of Reality and covers up the truth. **Kaffara** (II), also means to hide and cover, but in the context of making amends; hence **kaffārah** is an expiation or reparation.

*La`an* – Curse. From **la`ana**, to curse, damn, execrate. **Lā`ana** (III) is to utter an oath of condemnation. **Mal`ūn**, cursed, troublesome, naughty.

Lahw – Diversion, amusement, frivolous play. From **lahā**, to amuse (so as to forget), pass or kill time, to fritter away; to try to forget, become oblivious.

Lubb – Innermost, core, kernel, essence. In man it is his self-substance, the choicest part of him. From **labba**, to remain, abide, ripen into a kernel; to be or become possessed of understanding.

Hence **ūlū 'l-albāb** means those possessed of inner understanding. **Lubb** is purer than `aql (qv.) because it is not subject to cupidity or lust.

Makr – Cunning, craftiness; deception, plot. From **makara** to practise deceit, circumvent secretly, deceive, mislead. **Makkār** is a crafty or wily person. The **makr** of Allah is granting man respite or delay so as to enable him to accomplish his worldly aims.

*Ma`rifah* – Gnosis, realization, knowledge on which all knowledge rests. From `**arafa**, to know, recognize, differentiate, perceive. The `**ārif**, the gnostic, is who never sees anything but that he sees Allah in it, before it and after it.

*Ma`ruf* – Known, universally accepted; that which is good, beneficial; kindness, fairness. Enjoining good (**amr bil-ma`rūf**) is incumbent on every Muslim, as is forbidding evil (qv. **munkar**). From same root as **ma`rifah**.

Mawt – Death. From **māta**, to die, perish, abate, subside. Divine Name: **al-Mumīt**, the Creator of death.

Muhsin – See **ihsān**.

Mu'min – See **īmān**.

Munkar – Denied, detestable, not recognized, disallowed, unlawful. The opposite to **ma`rūf** (qv.) and obligatory for all the muslims to actively forbid (**nahī `an al-munkar**). From **nakira** (I), not to know, be ignorant, deny, feel repugnance towards; **ankara** (IV) to pretend not to know, disavow.

Muslim – See **islām**.

Nabī – (pl. **anbiyā'**) Prophet (*pbuh*); he who acquaints or informs mankind. From **naba'a** (I) to be exalted or elevated to announce, to utter a low sound; **naba'a** (II), to inform, make known. **Naba'** is news, announcement. **Nubūwwah** is Prophethood, as distinct from messengership (qv. **rasūl**). See Suras **al-Nabā'** and **al-Anbiyā'**.

Nadhīr – Warner, forerunner. From **nadhara** (I) to dedicate, consecrate, vow, (in the passive) be on one's guard against; and **andhara** (IV) to warn, caution, announce. **Nadhr** is a vow or pledge.

Nafs – Self, soul, psyche, mind, human being. The **nafs** includes man's innate nature, his genetic predisposition and conditioned behavior. Its manifestation may be base or animalistic, or spiritually elevated, according to the state of its purity. From **nafasa** (I), to be precious, valuable; **naffasa** (II) to comfort, relieve, air, uncover; **tanaffasa** (V), to breathe, pause for rest.

Nār – Fire; gunfire, conflagration. From **nawwara** (II), to flower, blossom, illuminate, fill with light; **anwara** (IV), to illuminate, elucidate, come to light. **Nār al-jahannam**, fire of Hell; **nawr**, blossom; **tanwīr**, blossoming.

Nashr – Unfolding, spreading out, announcement. **Yawm al-nashr**, the day of Resurrection. From **nashara** to scatter, disperse (sheep and goats after confining them in their resting place at night); expand, unfold, spread or publish (news). **Nushūr**, bringing to life, resurrection.

Nasr – Help, aid, support, victory. From **nasara**, to Help, render victorious; deliver, protect, save. **Nāsir**, supporter, protector; **ansār** (pl.), helpers, friends, the Madinan Muslims who gave refuge to the Prophet (*pbuh*) and followers after **hijrah** (qv.).

Nūr – Light, ray of brightness, illumination, glow. From same root as **nār** (qv.). **Munīr**, luminous. See **Ayat al-Nūr** (verse of light) in **Surat al-Nūr**. Divine Name: **al-Nūr**, the Light, which makes the perceptible seen.

Nifāq – Hypocrisy. From **nafaqa** (I), to spend, sell, to come out of a hole. **Nāfaqa** (III), to dissemble, enter into a hole from which there are 10 or 12 other entrances. **Anfaqa** (IV), to spend, expend (money). **Nafaq** is a hole or tunnel from which there is another exit (6:35).

Nuzul – Descent (as in revelation); that which is prepared for a guest, a gift. From **nazala** (I), to descend; **nazzala** (II), to send down, reveal. **Tanzīl**, revelation (qv.) (36:5).

Qadā' – Destiny, divine decree, conclusion, fulfilment, final judgement. From **qadā**, to settle, conclude, consummate, accomplish, fix, determine, decree.

Qadr – Divine or creational decree, measure, value, power, extent, scope, scale. From **qadara** (I), to decree, ordain, decide, possess power and ability, to be master of. Divine Name: **al-Qādir**, the All-Powerful.

Qalb – Heart; middle centre, core. From **qalaba**, to turn, turn around, about, down, up. **Qallaba** (II), to turn, transform, transmute, tilt. **Inqilāb**, revolution.

Qarīn – Intimate companion, associate. From **qarana** (I), to join, one thing to another; **qārana** (III) to become someone's companion, to associate. **Qarn** means generation (i.e. equal in age) and horn, or the part of the head of a human being which in an animal would be the place from where the horns grow. See **raqīb** and **shāhid**.

Rabb – Lord, master. From **rabba** (I), to be lord and master and **rabbaba**(II), to raise, bring up. **Rubūbīyyah**, lordship, is that attribute of Allah that brings up his subject, man, to fulfil his potential. The contract of **alastu bi-rabbikum** ('Am I not your Lord?') demands that the slave fulfils his part through `**ubūdīyyah** (qv.).

Raqīb – Watcher, observer, guardian. Nothing is hidden to the **raqīb**. From **raqaba** (I), to observe, respect, watch, wait; **rāqaba** (III), watch attentively, fear (Allah). **Murāqabah** therefore is self-watching by which one guards against wrong actions of the self. **Raqabah** or **riqab**, neck, slave, person. See **qarīn** and **shāhid**.

Rasūl – Messenger, (pl. **rusul**) apostle; those prophets who came with revelatory message, e.g. Moses, David, Jesus, Muhammad. From **rasala** (I), to send a messenger; **arsala** (IV), send out, transmit, set free.

Rizq – Provision, livelihood, sustenance, blessing. **Rizq** is anything from which one benefits. From **razzaqa**, to provide with means of sustenance (said of Allah); to bestow, endow, bless. Divine Name: **al-Razzāq**, the Sustainer.

Rūh – Spirit, (pl. **arwāh**) soul, breath of life. From **rāha**, to go away, to set out to do; **rawwaha** to refresh, animate. **Rūh** is spirit, which is subtle, while **nafs** is self, which is rigid. **Rūhāni**, pertaining to **rūh**.

*Rukū`* – Bowing (in prayer). From **raka`a** to have the back bent, to bow down. **Rukū`** is the courtesy that permits the nearness of **sujūd** (qv.).

Sabīl – Way, road, path; what is open, wherein is easiness. From **sabbala** (II), to assign (revenue) to charitable purpose in the way of Allah. **Ibn al-sabīl**, a traveller (lit. son of the road); **fī sabīl Allah**, in the way of Allah.

Sabr – Patience, steadfastness, forbearance (with oneself, others, and with the decree of Allah). From **sabara**, to bind, to endure patiently, to be constant towards. Divine Name: **al-Sabūr**, the Most Patient (see 8:46).

Sadr – Chest, (pl. **sudūr**) bosom, breast; front part, commander. From **sadara** (I), to return from watering, proceed, originate, stem; **saddara** (II) to send off, publish, introduce.

Salāt – Prayer, blessing, supplication. From **sala** (I), to strike the middle part of the back; **salla** (II) to pray, bend down in worship; **aslā** (IV) (of a mare foaling) rear haunches bending.

Salāt from Allah is mercy, **salāt** from the Angels is seeking forgiveness, **salāt** from the believers is supplication, **salāt** from birds and animals is glorification. **Salāt** can only be for goodness, while **du`ā** (qv.) could also be for evil.

Sālih – One who is good, sound, free from blemish; the person of integrity. The opposite of **fāsid** (qv. **fasād**). From **salaha** (I), to be right, honest, thrive; **sallaha** (II), to put in order; **sālaha** (III) to make peace; **aslaha** (IV) to make whole or sound. **Sālihāt** are good works, the antithesis of ruin and corruption.

Sawm – Fasting; the fast of Ramadan, one of the main duties of Muslims along with **salāt, hajj, zakāt, jihād, amr bi'l-ma`rūf wa al-nahī `an al-munkar** (qv.), which are undertaken according to the levels of **sharī`ah, tarīqah** and **haqīqah** (qv.)

Shāhid – Witness, from **shahida**, to be present at, to witness, bear testimony. The **shahādah** is the testimony or bearing witness that there is no God but Allah and that Muhammad is the Messenger of Allah. **Mashhūd** is that which is witnessed. Divine Name: **al-Shahīd**, the Witnesser of all things.

*Sharī`ah* – Revealed law or code of conduct; watering hole. From **shara`a**, to begin, enter, introduce, prescribe (laws). **Shāri`** means road; **mashra`**, spring. It is the complement and container of **haqīqah**, for the waters that gush from Reality's spring cannot be contained or drunk except from a fitting vessel.

Shawq – Yearning, longing, desire. From **shāqa** (I), to give joy, fill with longing.

Shirk – Association with or seeing other-than-Allah with Allah, idolatry. From **sharika**, to share, participate, associate. The **mushrik** perpetuates this association, ascribing a portion of Allah's power to others.

Shukr – Giving thanks, gratitude; acknowledging thanks by tongue and deed and heart. From **shakara**, to give thanks. **Shukr** is the opposite state of **kufr** (qv.).

Sidq – Truthfulness, sincerity, veracity, correctness. From **sadaqa**, to speak the truth, be sincere, give alms, the **sādiq** is he who is true.

Sirr – Secret, inmost, heart, mystery, underlying reason. From **sarra**, to make happy, gladden, delight; to confide or keep a secret.

Sujūd – Prostration in prayer, adoration. **Sujūd** is the position of nearness. From **sajada**, to be humble, submit oneself, bend down in adoration. **Sajjada** (II) is used of a camel bending down to be mounted. **Masjid** is the place of prostration, hence a mosque.

Taqwā – Precautious, fearful awareness of (obedience to) Allah; devoutness, godliness. From **waqā** (I), to guard, to preserve, shield, prevent (a danger); and **ittaqā** (VIII), to beware, be on one's guard, protect oneself. The **muttaqī** is he who acts by *taqwā*.

Tarīqah – The way; manner, mode or means. The middle way between **sharī'ah** and **haqīqah**. From **taraqa**, to knock, forge, reach. The Prophet (*pbuh*) said: **sharī'ah** is my word, **tarīqah** my act and **haqīqah** my state.

Tawbah – Repentance, turning away from wrong action. From **tāba**, to turn (to Allah), hence to repent. Divine Name: **al-Tawwāb**, the Constantly Returning with Mercy. There are three parts to **tawbah**: turning away from wrong action, self-rebuke, return to Allah.

Tawhīd – Divine unity, union; belief in and understanding of Allah's oneness. From **wahada**, to be alone, singular, unique, unmatched, without equal. Divine Names: **al-Wāhid**, the One and **al-Ahad**, the Unique One.

Wafā' – Fulfillment, redemption (of a promise), loyalty, fidelity. From **wafā**, to be perfect, complete, to live up to e.g. a promise). **Wafāh** means death.

Wird – Lit. a place of descent, especially to water for the purpose of drinking; special **dhikr** to unlock, self-awakening, recited according to the shaykh's instruction. From **warida**, to be present, arrive at, to water.

Yaqīn – Certainty. From **yaqina**, to be certain. **Yaqīn** has three parts; **'Ilm al-yaqīn**, the knowledge of certainty; **'ayn al-yaqīn**, the eye of certainty; **haqq al-yaqīn**, the source of certainty.

Zakāt – Purity, a portion of one's wealth or substance given in order to purify the rest, hence alms tax. From **zakiya**, to grow; be pure or purified.

Zuhd – Doing without. Not necessarily asceticism, because the **zāhid** does not desire or need what he does without, so no denial is involved. From **zahida**, to abstain from, abandon, withdraw, renounce.

www.ingramcontent.com/pod-product-compliance
Lightning Source LLC
Chambersburg PA
CBHW071216090426
42736CB00014B/2842